THE SCHOLAR-FRIENDS

THE
SCHOLAR-FRIENDS

LETTERS OF FRANCIS JAMES CHILD
AND JAMES RUSSELL LOWELL

Edited by
M. A. DEWOLFE HOWE
and
G. W. COTTRELL, JR

GREENWOOD PRESS, PUBLISHERS
WESTPORT, CONNECTICUT

INTRODUCTORY NOTE

THE dual editorship of this book calls for explanation. 'The Scholar-Friends,' in an earlier form, was prepared by the first, and senior, of the two editors named on the title-page. His purpose was to make Francis James Child, through his letters to James Russell Lowell, better known not so much to specialists in English scholarship as to the literate 'general reader.' Lowell's qualities as a letter-writer were already so familiar, through the abundant publication of his correspondence, that relatively few of his letters to Child seemed essential to the immediate purpose.

When the manuscript of this shorter 'Scholar-Friends' was submitted for publication in the *Harvard Library Bulletin*, its editor, whose name now appears as second editor on the foregoing title-page, suggested extending the material by presenting both sides of the correspondence between Child and Lowell. There were good reasons for pursuing this course, especially on the ground that it would link the friendship of the two men more closely with their scholarship. The considerable task of enlargement and rearrangement seemed formidable to a senior editor, but if a younger hand and eye were ready to undertake it, why indeed should it not be done? The four instalments of 'The Scholar-Friends,' first printed in the *Harvard Library Bulletin*, and now offered in this book printed from the same types, represent the joiner-work of the junior editor in making a consistent whole of what the senior editor had already done and of his own extensive additions and elucidations. The result must speak for itself. Senior and junior editor are at one in accepting the responsibilities, with whatever consequences, of their collaboration. May it be added that this collaboration has caused the senior editor to regard the junior as indeed his own 'scholar-friend?'

THE SCHOLAR-FRIENDS

THE SCHOLAR-FRIENDS

LETTERS OF FRANCIS JAMES CHILD
AND JAMES RUSSELL LOWELL

OWN through the ages letters have been the great preservative of personality. The man who writes them cannot help revealing himself. Nor does it stop there. The tone and spirit of his letters vary with the natures of the friends to whom he is writing, and, though of course less obviously, the personality of each friend is suggested if not actually revealed.

The pages that follow speak, with this reciprocal illumination, for the friendship of two Harvard scholars, Francis James Child and James Russell Lowell. Lowell's eminent place among English letter-writers has long been established, through the printing of large numbers of his letters to his friends and to his daughter. Not so with Child. Only one small collection of Child's letters, *A Scholar's Letters to a Young Lady*, issued in 1920 in a limited edition, has shown the quality of his correspondence.

The ten opening pages of that little book, edited by the senior editor of the present volume, were devoted to a biographical sketch, 'Francis James Child.' It would be superfluous to repeat in this place the main facts of his life and work — facts that may now be gathered in greater detail with the aid of the bibliography following the article on Child in the *Dictionary of American Biography*. The peculiar charm of Child's letters has impressed more than one reader. Among the published *Letters* of Gamaliel Bradford is one which he wrote to the senior editor immediately on reading the *Letters to a Young Lady*. 'I am rather an epicure in letters,' he said, 'having made a business as well as a pleasure of them for a great many years, and I do not know of any American letters that are superior to these, if any equal.' [1] A few years later, having been given access to other letters of Child's, including a

---

[1] The recipient of these letters wished at the time of their publication to be nameless, and her wish was observed. She may now be identified as the late Miss Emily Tuckerman of Stockbridge, Massachusetts.

number to Lowell, he wrote to Mrs Gilbert Campbell Scoggin, Child's daughter, in a similar vein of appreciation, saying, 'It does seem to me that a book with the title "Letters of James Russell Lowell and Francis James Child" ought to attract notice, and, notice once attracted, no one could fail to read with interest and delight.'

Here was an implied challenge to do something about it. Many circumstances have deferred action until this late day. In the meanwhile, considerable numbers of Child letters to Lowell and of Lowell to Child had been placed in the Harvard College Library by Mrs Scoggin. Not quite untouched,[2] this correspondence now seems — in view of the enlarged conception of the present undertaking — deserving of publication substantially in its entirety, for its testimonial to a warm and rich friendship between two highly gifted men and for its vivid conveying of personality. Child's letters, covering, in the very nature of things, a far wider range of interest than those addressed to a 'Young Lady,' yet couched in similarly sensitive, humorous, affectionate terms, clearly explain his place among his contemporaries as a uniquely beloved man and scholar, while greatly reinforcing his claim to high epistolary rank. Those of Lowell, though obviously of less significance in view of the extent of his correspondence already published, nevertheless have seemed worthy of inclusion here, not only as foils for and explanations of the Child letters, but because of their own intrinsic merit. However brief (and they are usually briefer than Child's) they yet invariably contain some flash of their writer's wit or charm.

Not the least striking feature of this correspondence is its revelation of the dynamic course of a friendship, from its first formal overtures to its final intimate close. Salutations range from 'Dear Sir' and 'My dear Lowell (if you will allow me to call you so)' to 'Carissimo Ciarli,'[3] 'Dearest Jamie,' 'Deliciae Meae,' and 'Carissimum Caput.' Subscriptions run similarly from 'Yours faithfully' to 'Ever your most affectionate.' And all this rich development is seen against a background of life's stages from ascendant young manhood through the strains and

[2] Four of the Lowell letters to Child (14 April 1878, 30 December 1879, 2 February 1883, December 1883) were printed — with important omissions, be it said — by Norton in his *Letters of James Russell Lowell* (Boston, 1893; revised edition 1904), and Bradford quoted a few characteristic sentences from Child's letters to Lowell in his 'portrait' of Child in *As God Made Them* (Boston, 1929).

[3] 'Ciarli' being the transcription of an Italian beggar's attempt to pronounce 'Child.'

heart searchings of the middle years to the hard-won serenity of old age. Particularly memorable is the quality of the late evening light that plays over the last letters.

Another facet is that of the *scholar*-friends.' Child's pre-eminence in scholarship has been the theme of numerous panegyrics, centering about his monumental achievement in the *English and Scottish Popular Ballads.* Here we see him in the midst of his unceasing hunt for ballads or in the stern pursuit of verbal parallels, yet delighting no less in the humors of scholarship, ever ready for a pun, a quip, a quotation. Lowell the scholar has been overshadowed by Lowell the poet, the essayist, the diplomat, and rightly so; yet in these letters he exhibits again and again a familiarity and concern with the minutiae of research that certainly are not ordinarily associated with his career. Each appreciated to the full the special virtues of the other, and each was ever ready to further without hint of rivalry the aims of the other. One thinks of Lowell's praise of Child's lectures at Johns Hopkins, of Child's constructive criticism of Lowell's essay on Chaucer, of Lowell, again, ballad-hunting in Child's behalf.

Implicit in these letters, too, is the love of reading and of books. In fact the entire correspondence might be said to have reading as one of its cornerstones — reading and collecting. Concern for the Harvard Library is a recurrent theme, and both Child and Lowell were among the great benefactors of the Library. Certain aspects of Lowell's contribution have previously been noticed in the pages of the *Harvard Library Bulletin.*[4] As for Child, a minute adopted by the Library Council 1 November 1897, a year after his death, bears such eloquent witness that it is quoted here in full:

This minute was read and adopted at the meeting of the Library Council of Harvard University, November 1, 1897: —

Professor Francis James Child became a member of the old Library Committee (the predecessor of the Council) at the time of its organization in 1859. In 1865 he was chosen Secretary of the Committee, and on April 6, 1867, when the newly established Council of the Library had its first meeting, he was elected Secretary, an office which he held until his death in September, 1896. Until recent years the regular duties of the Council included many matters of detail, and meetings were held more frequently than at the present time. Yet Professor Child was constant in his attendance, since the records show that he was absent from only four meetings during the thirty-two years from 1864 to 1896.

[4] Francis M. Rogers, 'The Libraries for Romance Languages and Literatures,' *Harvard Library Bulletin,* IV (1950), 271–276.

This assiduity was not, however, the greatest of his services to the Library. Besides his general interest in all the duties of the Council, the value of his work as a selector of books cannot be over-estimated. His own studies covered a wide range, and at the time of his death he was a director of expenditures for books on the English language and literature, Folk-lore, Italian and Romance languages, Mediaeval literature, Portuguese and Spanish, Scandinavian literature, and Slavic languages and literature.

Moreover it is due to his researches and recommendations that the Library possesses a collection of Ballad literature, including manuscripts, which is unrivalled anywhere in the world. The Folk-lore collection, too, is wonderfully complete for all periods, and if not unequalled, is certainly one of the best in existence, even Slavic Folk-lore being represented. The collection of Mediaeval literature of all nations forms an excellent working library, hardly to be surpassed at any University except in such large collections as the Bodleian.

For all these the University is mainly indebted to Professor Child's loyal and indefatigable exertions. The frequenters of the Library will long miss him in his accustomed place before the little table at the East end of the old Stack, and the members of the Council deeply mourn the loss of one who was wise, far-seeing, and unselfish in his consideration of every department of learning with which the Library is concerned.

A true copy of the Record
[signed] Morris H. Morgan
Secretary of the Council [5]

The correspondence is accordingly given in its entirety, except for a very few purely formal and quite unimportant pieces. Lowell letters to Child already printed in part by Norton are published here in full, from the originals. The only other published letter of Lowell to Child, actually the first in the series, is also included, for the sake of completeness, but in this case it is merely reprinted from the previously published version, since the original is no longer available. The letters are printed with hardly an omission (although a few doubtful passages remain, where Child's infamous hand has resisted the most earnest attempts at decipherment), and orthography, punctuation, and arrangement all reflect the originals.

An attempt has been made also to arrange the letters in chronological order, and to provide a modicum of framework (elaborate stage-setting and annotation would obviously contradict the spirit of the correspondence). The frequently inadequate dating — a sure sign

[5] Printed from a copy sent Mrs Child (and included among the Child papers presented by Mrs Scoggin), with the signature of Morris Hicky Morgan, then Assistant Professor of Latin, later Professor of Classical Philology, and himself a major benefactor of the Library through his great collection of Persius.

that a writer of letters has no thought of their consideration in relation to the course of his own life — can often be supplemented by internal evidence, and occasionally an undated letter can thus be absolutely fixed, but even after a considerable amount of detective work a fair proportion of the letters remain very tentatively placed and may in some cases be several years out of proper order.

Lowell, born in 1819, was six years older than Child, and eight years his senior as a graduate of Harvard. At the time of the first known letter, Lowell had lately dazzled his contemporaries with that *annus mirabilis* which saw the appearance of *Poems: Second Series*, *A Fable for Critics*, *The Biglow Papers* (first series), *The Vision of Sir Launfal*, and some forty contributions to periodicals. His interests as writer and editor gave him, in spite of his close association with Cambridge, a concern with Boston and outlying *partes infidelium* that did not characterize the academic circle, and no doubt his relations with Child were no less official or semi-official than the form and tone of this letter would imply. Child, since his graduation in 1846, had been tutor and instructor at Harvard, in such diverse subjects as mathematics, rhetoric, and political economy. He presumably left for his two years of study in Europe shortly after receiving this letter. The 'compliment' here alluded to and declined by Lowell was an invitation to deliver the Phi Beta Kappa poem at Harvard in 1850; the actual poet of the occasion was Bayard Taylor, who became Lowell's guest at Elmwood for the time.

Plate I reproduces a drawing of Child in German student costume, executed in Göttingen in 1850 or 1851, and presented by Child to Joseph T. Atkinson, of Baltimore, who in turn gave it to Harvard, where it is now to be found in the University Archives. Beneath the drawing runs an inscription in Child's hand:

> Ein starkes Bier, ein beizender Toback,
> Und eine Magd im Putz, das ist von mein[?] Geschmack.
> F. J. C. seinem J. T. A.

The opening letter in the correspondence of the scholar-friends reads as follows:

Elmwood, 1 Oct, 1849.

Dear Sir, — with many thanks for the compliment implied in your selection, I must beg leave to decline performing the service which you request of me.

5

But, now that I have you by the button, allow me to make a suggestion in behalf of my guild. Should not the "Literary Committee" take it into consideration that the attentive capacities of an audience are limited? Either so tether the orators that they shall neither graze upon nor trample that share of the common paddock which belongs of right to Pegasus, or (as turn and turn about is fair play) let orator and poet have the first place in alternate years. Do the orators believe that the ears of their audience are so long that a certain amount of wooden talk is needful by way of handle, as it were, in order to make the *point* of their discourse reach down to the tympanum? Certain it is that, if the hearers had their way, the poet would literally find, on most occasions, a clear stage and no favor. For there is a certain point of time (say quarter past 2 o'clock) at which they become instinctively satisfied that their dinner is cooked and cooling, and after that one might as well recite verses to the men whose heads do grow beneath their shoulders, and whose ears consequently are in their bellies, or to the akephali, who must have no ears at all. This crisis may come a trifle earlier with country members, and later with those from the city, but a series of observations has convinced me that quarter past two is a fair average.

Year after next, let the poet come first, and let the selection be honestly made with a special eye to avenging the wrongs of our "oppressèd race." Choose some author of "Washington, an Epic," with an eighteen inch bore, some McHenry wont to graduate his verses by the longaeval scale of the Antediluvians, let him be dined amply beforehand by subscription of poets who have come in to the nutshells and melonrinds of former anniversaries, and then let him turn ad libitum the crank of his pitiless and unweariable barrelorgan. Would he not seem to tower up into a grim figure of Nemesis?

With this for your private consideration, should you be on the Committee next year,

            I remain,

                Very sincerely yours

                      J. R. Lowell [6]

The first known letters from Child to Lowell are to be dated from January 1855, yet there must have been a considerable prior interchange, for during 1854 Lowell's editions of Keats, Dryden, and Wordsworth had appeared in the *British Poets* series, published by Little, Brown, the general editorship of which Child had undertaken in 1852. None the less, these letters suggest the opening passages of a

---

[6] Reprinted from *New Letters of James Russell Lowell*, ed. M. A. DeWolfe Howe (New York, 1932), pp. 33–34, with the kind permission of the publishers, Harper & Brothers.

warmer acquaintance. They obviously relate to the course of Lowell Institute lectures, on English poets, which Lowell began 9 January 1855 and which had so signal a success. In these years, it may be noted, men still remembered Jackson's victory at New Orleans, 8 January 1813. Did not Lowell similarly, and as late as 8 January 1867, date a letter to Edmund Quincy 'Die Sanct: And: Nov. Aurel:'? [7] Subsequent references to the volume of Skelton indicate its use in the editing of that poet for the Little, Brown series; the *British Poets* edition duly appeared in 1856, based on the edition of Dyce with revisions and additions by Child.

'Dr Howe' is Estes Howe, husband of Lois White Howe, the sister of Lowell's first wife, Maria White Lowell, who had died in 1853. Mabel Lowell, the only surviving child of the marriage, stayed with the Howes, at their home on 'Professors' Row,' Cambridge, while Lowell was abroad 1855–56 (see below). Frances Dunlap, of Portland, Maine, whom Lowell married in September 1857, acted as governess for Mabel during this period. 'Fanny' Lowell figures largely in the later correspondence with Child. There were no children by the second marriage.

Plate II (from a photograph in the Harvard Archives) shows Child the Young Professor. On his return from Europe in 1851 he had been made Boylston Professor of Rhetoric and Oratory, a chair which he held until 1876. Routine duties of this chair, such as the supervision of large quantities of student themes, though performed by Child with unfailing devotion and good nature, greatly delayed the accomplishment of his major work.

Monday 8 Jan [1855]

My dear Lowell (if you will allow me to call you so)

I do not write, as you may suppose, to celebrate the glorious memory of the battle of New Orleans, but first to wish you speed in the emprise which begins tomorrow, and principally to ask for two tickets to the evening lectures in case any should be still left in your hands. In this application I do not expect any success, knowing well that the Bostoniennes are ready to tear you in pieces as small as Orpheus. But an intelligent young woman wrote to me to obtain at least one if I could, and I could not do less than try. I shall recommend her to the afternoon course. I have heard the best

[7] *New Letters of James Russell Lowell*, p. 119.

things of your prolusion at Shady Hill and hope to indulge my own ears with the sound of your voice.

I am preparing a hecatomb for tomorrow evening

Yours faithfully

F. J. Child

J. R. Lowell Esq

[Cambridge, 19 or 26 January 1855]

My dear Lowell,

I have left Master Skelton for you at Dr Howe's, and would have brought it to Elmwood had time and the state of the tides between me & you allowed. I am off tomorrow for New York, and must depend on the Advertiser for my lectures. But I hope to get back in time to witness the Grand Principal Act of the last, and to celebrate your triumph at Shady Hill or elsewhere. Take my parting blessing & believe me always

Yours faithfully

F J Child

Friday

As early as 31 January 1855 Longfellow recorded in his journal that Lowell was to succeed him in the Smith Professorship of the French and Spanish Languages and Literatures.[8] Child, not aware that the matter was already settled, wrote from New York to urge Lowell to accept. Among the terms was the provision that Lowell should have a year abroad to fit himself more fully for his new duties. Before he sailed, in June 1855, and following the conclusion of the Lowell lectures, he made an unrewarding but hardly unrewarded lecture tour in the West. His edition of Donne's *Poetical Works* appeared in the British Poets series in this year.

New York, 7 Feb^{ry} [1855]

My dear Lowell,

I heard last evening from Norton of the overtures made you by the Corporation (a matter I had been wishing to speak with you about, having had some words with Dr Walker on the subject) and that you were inclined to listen to terms. I had not supposed they would take any steps to fill the place immediately, or I should have endeavored to prepossess you in favor of it. We are all interested in your accepting the nomination, for

---

[8] Samuel Longfellow, *Life of Henry Wadsworth Longfellow* (Boston, 1891), II, 281.

PLATE I

CHILD THE GERMAN STUDENT

PLATE II

CHILD THE YOUNG PROFESSOR

PLATE IIIb
GRACE NORTON

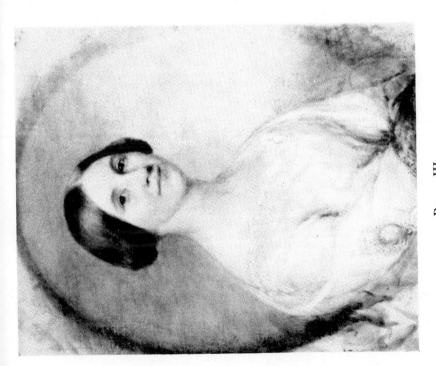

PLATE IIIa
JANE NORTON

PLATE IV

LOWELL AT ELMWOOD, CA. 1865

a thousand reasons, and among them are the credit of the College in the land, your own happiness, and our personal pleasure at having you associated with us. Were it not a goodly sight to see you with the graybeards around the council board, meting out justice to rowdy Sophomores and in the course of an inquisition into the cause of broken windows referring with pious enthusiasm to your good old days under President Saturn when such immoralities[?] were unknown? The pleasure of attending Faculty meetings is alone worth more than the price of admission, I assure you. Then think of what is implied in your Lectureship. Lying on the sofa and reading Don Quixote, Reineke Fuchs, Dante & the Nibelungen, Troubadours, & Contes Joyaux. No teaching of grammars, no reading La Fontaine & Iriarte with all the blockheads in a class — but the privilege of free speech on the great themes of modern literature. By coming in with us too you secure two vacations a year, which you have not had I suppose since you left college, and if you don't get much money, you at any rate acquire the right of feeling that you belong to one of the disinterested & liberal classes of society to whom money is no object, and another "inalienable" one of grumbling once a year at the stinginess of the Americans to their greatest men. There are many other advantages which might be enumerated of all the various kinds that have been mentioned. I am sorry that you do not feel in the highest spirits at the thought of abandoning a Bedouin for a steady life. Take our word for it, that you will find the yoke a light one and when you find what deep rut furrows you can turn up you will enjoy ploughing in harness

I am actually in the fruition of some of these pleasures which I hold out to you — having nothing to do these few weeks but read Dante, Don Quixote & Faust in most agreeable company. Your lectures are read with great delight by my friends here when they can get hold of them. You ought to give them in New York after you have concluded your other engagements. — I am in a hurry this morning and have been somewhat distracted while writing these lines But I hope that I have said enough to convince you of the sincere pleasure with which I should embrace you as a colleague and of my strong conviction not only that you would distinguish yourself in your office but enjoy this new kind of activity.

Quod felix faustumque sit!

Yours most faithfully

F. J. Child

J. R. Lowell Esq

I did not discover that this was a fragment of a sheet until too late.

[Cambridge, March, 1855]

My dear Lowell,

I expected to see you last night at the play and indeed in your new character you ought especially to have been present. The Nortons are

9

the only people who have seen you since you were obliged to hide your-self from popular applause in some country village. I hope however to get one glimpse of you before you leave America, if not before you begin your western triumph.

My immediate object (no doubt you foresaw I was coming to some-thing) is to ask you to leave Skelton somewhere for me. The copy from which we are printing is defective to the extent of a whole signature. I am going over the notes to see if I can better them, but it is a bootless labor. What are the British Poets to do without you, do you think?

Ever faithfully yours

F. J Child

James Russell Lowell Esq.

Elmwood, 12th March 1855.

5 o'clock A.M.

My dear Child,

I should have answered your kind letter from New York long ago — but that I heard just after receiving it that you had gone from there & assumed a nomadic address. Since your coming back I have called upon you (or your door) twice & failed — that is, I found the door.

You see my unheard of date. I start for Buffalo this morning at 7 — I faithfully corrected the last copy for Donne yesterday. Skelton I left for you at Mrs Dr Howe's — not being able to find you. Many thanks for him. I would sooner endorse Dyce's notes than 'take them up' as you speak of doing. There are too many of em & he has sometimes if I remem-ber rightly gone back to an old reading which means nothing but that the scribe could not spell. But they are learned.

A man writing at five o'clock in the morning cannot be expected to know anything except that he ought to be in bed & I will only add that I shall hope to see you as soon as I get back from the West & to thank you for your kind letter.

About the Professorship, I am doubtful if I was wise to accept.

Very truly yours

J. R. Lowell.

Prof. Child.

The next three letters remain unanchored. The first two volumes of Gruntvig's great work, *Danmarks gamle Folkeviser*, which in many respects was the inspiration of Child's *magnum opus*, appeared in parts 1852–56; publication of the third volume was completed in 1862, and of the fourth in 1883. The Gruntvig-Child correspondence [9] clearly indicates the share Gruntvig had in the molding of *The English and Scottish Popular Ballads* while it reveals a charming personal relation between the two foremost scholars of the general field.

Child's 'lovely pupils at Shady Hill' are presumably Jane and Grace Norton, sisters of Charles Eliot, and intimate friends and correspondents of both Child and Lowell. In a letter to Grace written from Stockbridge 12 February 1860 Child compliments her on the German exercise she had just sent him.[10] At Stockbridge, as in New York, during these midwinter vacation trips, Child visited the Robert Sedgwick family, whose daughter Elizabeth he married (at Stockbridge) on 20 August 1860.

Portraits of Jane and Grace Norton are reproduced in Plate III, that of the former from a miniature by Staigg in the possession of Mrs William Norton Bullard, that of the latter from a crayon sketch by Rowse now in the Worcester Art Museum. Both are reproduced with the kind permission of the owners.

[ca. 1857?]

Prepare the minds of your family and friends for a separation until Saturday, dear Lowell. For he that arrives — as you will and I shall — at 4½, and goes at 8 the next morning, may "exclaim" with the Roman emperor hunc perdidi diem. Now a diem we may perhaps afford to lose — but $4.00 — 40 díms are not to be thrown away. You must therefore either come in the evening boat, starting (from Fall River or Old Colony Station) at 5 & arriving at 9 — or else you must starting at 11½ tomorrow stay till Saty —

Dixi.

F. C.   Before breakfast.

Monday. [January? 1860?]

Dear Lowell,

I send the Scandinavian catalogue you said you wanted & lists of books which I consider desirable. — nearly all volkslieder & volksmärchen. The only thing dear I have put into the lists is the Wiener Jahrbücher — indispensable to you & to me. Still *I* would rather have the ballad books first. Those which are in German Swedish & Danish I have marked with a cross as deserving preference. I have not filled out the lists properly for want of

[9] Published by S. B. Hustvedt in *Ballad Books and Ballad Men* (Cambridge, Mass., 1930), Appendix A.
[10] Among the Norton papers in the Harvard Library.

time to go to the Library. Eliot says the lists are to be completed by March 1. If I can have a day or two at the beginning of the term I will look up all the particulars of price & date. As for place they can all be found at Leipsic.

I wish I could leave you Svend Grundtvig for your leisure moments. I will try to get through with the two first vols in the course of the vacation. The collection of Nyerup which is in the Library may answer your general[?] purposes equally well, or perhaps you will prefer Arwidsson's Swedish ballads — they being well edited, and Nyerup's Danish not particularly so, (according to Grundtvig) I mean now sooner or later to make a clean sweep of the whole field, of *Northern* ballads at least.

Give my lovely pupils at Shady Hill a little help in German while I am gone. I hope to bring back good news and a light heart.

With kindest regards to your wife ever your faithful & affectionate

F. Ciarli.

Am hard pressed for time or I should come bodily.

Elmwood, 24th May. [186–?]

Carissimo mio Ciarli!

ho fatto il dovere da te imposto. Whether I have made the certificates ample enough? If not I will enlarge & intensify to order.

A fig for gardens! Potatoes are the real thing, & mine are six inches tall with no help from the sun. They laugh at Phibbus' car, having fire enough in their own bellies to serve their turn. Flowers are very well — but I am cutting my own asparagus. They may please an unregenerate nose — but I have lettuces as crisp & melting in the mouth as the first veneer of ice left pendent by a shrinking brook. Already I have cucumbers that more than match the orangetrees of Sorrento with fruit & flowers at once. My tomatoeses & eggplantses already flatten themselves against the glasses of the hotbeds, eager for larger fields. Still, I wish you all manner of success, & fancying you among your unreplenished beds, in which the seeds are hibernating, think of great Diocletian. I have seen pansies blooming just below the snow of Etna, & you may yet see a blossom or two on the southern edge of this estranged spring — if there should turn out to be one.

Meanwhile, I am lovingly yours

J R L

Among the Child papers presented to Harvard there is the following little poem in Lowell's hand. It is tempting to associate it with a gift of a copy of *Master Tyl Owlglass*, translated by K. R. H. Mackenzie and illustrated by 'Alfred Crowquill' (London: Trübner & Co., 1860; Boston, Ticknor & Fields, 1860). The London edition, interestingly enough, is advertised on the wrapper of the first part of *The Biglow Papers, Second Series*, published by Trübner in 1862. But there were of course other translations of *Tyl* of likely date, including that of Charles de Coster into French (Paris 1868), which has served as the basis for many of the popular editions of more recent times.

[186–?]

> Ciarli mio,
> Ti guardi Iddio!
> Ecco il libro moderno-vecchio
> Chiamato lo strige-specchio;
> Per darne una sentenza di botto,
> Potrei dirlo ben tradotto;
> Ritienilo quanto vuoi,
> Sempre contandomi frà i tuoi.

The next letter may be tentatively assigned to 1862, when parts of the second series of *The Biglow Papers* were appearing in the *Atlantic Monthly*. Child's lowness of spirits may well reflect the state of the country, deep in civil war by that year, and the soliciting of subscriptions may derive from the same source. It was the spring of 1862, it will be remembered, that saw the famous collaboration of Child and Lowell in *Il Pesceballo*, the burlesque operetta staged to raise money for war relief.[11] Also presumably to be assigned to 1862 is Lowell's anonymous contribution of 'A Compromise' to Child's *War-Songs for Freemen*, first published in that year.[12]

Finally, the memorable description of Child left by Henry James harks back specifically to 1862. It is so apposite that its quotation here cannot be resisted. James had just come up to Harvard from Newport to enter the Law School, and was boarding with his brother William at Mrs Upham's, where Child was also temporarily a patron:

The image most vividly restored is doubtless that of Professor F. J. Child, head of the "English Department" at Harvard and master of that great modern science of folk-lore to his accomplishment in which his vast and slowly-published

[11] See M. A. DeWolfe Howe, ' "Il Pesceballo": The Fishball Operetta of Francis James Child,' *New England Quarterly*, XXIII (1950), 187–199.

[12] These verses, to the tune of 'Duncan Gray,' have apparently not previously been identified as Lowell's — they are not to be found for example in *Uncollected Poems of James Russell Lowell*, ed. Thelma M. Smith (Philadelphia, 1950). However, a draft of the last stanza in Lowell's autograph and with autograph corrections, found among the Child papers presented by Mrs Scoggin, would seem to leave no doubt as to the authorship.

collection of the Ballad literature of our language is a recognised monument; delightful man, rounded character, passionate patriot, admirable talker, above all thorough humanist and humorist. He was the genial autocrat of that break-fast-table not only, but of our symposia otherwise timed, and as he comes back to me with the fresh and quite circular countenance of the time before the personal cares and complications of life had gravely thickened for him, his aspect *all* finely circular, with its close rings of the fairest hair, its golden rims of the largest glasses, its finished rotundity of figure and attitude, I see that *there* was the American spirit — since I was "after" it — of a quality deeply inbred, beautifully adjusted to all extensions of knowledge and taste and, as seemed to me, quite sublimely quickened by everything that was at the time so tremen-dously in question. That vision of him was never afterwards to yield to other lights — though these, even had occasion for them been more frequent with me, couldn't much have interfered with it; so that what I still most retain of him is the very flush and mobility, the living expansion and contraction, the bright comedy and almost lunar eclipse, of his cherubic face according as things ap-peared to be going for the country. I was always just across from him, as my brother, beside whom I took my place, had been, and I remember well how vivid a clock-face it became to me; I found still, as in my younger time, matter enough everywhere for gaping, but greatest of all, I think, while that tense sea-son lasted, was my wonder for the signs and portents, the quips and cranks, the wreathèd smiles, or otherwise the candid obscurations, of our prime talker's presented visage. I set, as it were, the small tick of my own poor watch by it — which private register would thump or intermit in agreement with these indica-tions. I recover it that, thanks to the perpetual play of his sympathy and irony, confidence and scorn, as well as to that of my own less certainly directed sensi-bility, he struck me on the bad days, which were then so many, as fairly august, cherubism and all, for sincerity of association with every light and shade, every ebb and flow, of our Cause.[13]

In the present letter, Child's homely use of 'lalocs' for 'lilacs' is as welcome as the survival of his versified response to Lowell would have been.

[1862?]

My dear Friend,

I owe you for three things, yea four — two poems and two lalocs. If the trees only could come up to the poetry, wouldn't I raise the price of this estate! I wish I could have heard the Biglow from your own mouth, more to have laughed out loud — which I rarely have spirits for — than for anything else. It will bear reading any number of times. I enclose a wretched attempt to answer you in your own style. I am sure you will

[13] *Notes of a Son and Brother* (New York, 1914), pp. 320–322, reprinted here with the kind permission of the publishers, Charles Scribner's Sons.

stop writing if this fellow follows you up: so I hope he may be choked by and for his first attempt.

The trees have taken kindly to the soil and don't show any sign of homesickness. I shall always feel as if you were near if they live.

The women of the Freedmen's Society gave me the names of certain persons whom I was to ask for subscriptions We have got about 640 dollars from the "College Chapel" — including all the people that dont go anywhere to church. I have assailed everybody but you, and now have neither conscience to ask you nor to let you go. You must consider in your giving that you may be called upon regularly for several years to come.

Always your affectionate

F J Child.

Prof Lowell.

No letter from either Lowell or Child alludes to that peak of Lowell's poetical endeavor, the *Commemoration Ode*, delivered at the special memorial exercises held by Harvard for its war dead 21 July 1865. But a record left by Lowell many years later is so aptly illustrative of the relation between the scholar-friends that it may well find a place here:

The ode itself was an improvisation. Two days before the Commemoration I had told my friend Child that it was impossible — that I was dull as a door-mat. But the next day something gave me a jog and the whole thing came out of me with a rush. I sat up all night writing it out clear, and took it on the morning of the day to Child. "I have something, but don't yet know what it is, or whether it will do. Look at it and tell me." He went a little way apart with it under an elm tree in the College yard. He read a passage here and there, brought it back to me, and said, "Do? I should think so! Don't you be scared." And I wasn't, but virtue enough had gone out of me to make me weak for a fortnight after.[14]

A photograph of Lowell, taken 1865 or 1866 at Elmwood by W. J. Stillman, is shown in Plate IV. It is reproduced from a print which once belonged to Oliver Wendell Holmes and is now in the Harvard Archives.

The next two letters, both from Lowell, are inserted in special,

[14] Lowell to Richard Watson Gilder, 16 January 1886, in *Letters of James Russell Lowell*, ed. C. E. Norton (Boston, 1904), III, 149. This and following quotations from the *Letters* are printed with the kind permission of the publishers, Houghton, Mifflin and Company.

large-paper copies, dated 1867, of *The Biglow Papers, Second Series* and *The Biglow Papers* (first series) respectively (both volumes presented to the Child Memorial Library at Harvard by Mr Gilbert Campbell Scoggin). The former volume is inscribed 'To F. J. Child, with the author's love, 25th May, 1867.', and has on the verso of the title-page, also in Lowell's hand, 'Twelve copies printed on large paper J. R. L. Number 2.'; the latter volume has merely 'To F J. C. with the love of J. R. L. 1867.'

The history of these large-paper *Biglows* has remained obscure. Chamberlain and Livingston in their bibliography of Lowell take no note of a large-paper first series, and attribute all three copies known to them to the second series (Longfellow and Norton copies at Harvard, Aldrich copy in the library of Thomas Bailey Aldrich).[15] Actually, only two copies of each series have at present been traced, all at Harvard: Aldrich and Child copies of the first series and Child and Longfellow copies of the second series; there is no record that a Norton copy of either series was ever at Harvard. The Child copies of the two volumes are illustrated in Plate V.

The 'copy of Sir Launfal' for Mrs Child would have been of the edition illustrated by S. Eytinge, Jr, dated 1867 but ready as early as November 1866.

In the second letter, Lowell alludes to Child's epoch-making 'Observations on the Language of Chaucer,' communicated to the American Academy of Arts and Sciences 3 June 1862 and printed in Volume VIII (1863), new series, of the *Memoirs* of the Academy (a few preprints being available for private distribution in September 1862). This paper of Child's has been regarded as the foundation of modern Chaucerian scholarship.

Elmwood, 5th Decr 1866.

Caro mio Ciarli,

I at last return your "Fabliaux." I fear I should hardly have reached this pitch of virtue, had I not succeeded in buying a nice copy which I found on Penington's Catalogue at $12 — full bound in old calf. Not dear?

I wish to subscribe for three tickets to the parlor concerts.

I do not know whether I told you that the reason you have had no copy of

---

[15] J. C. Chamberlain (assisted by L. S. Livingston), *A Bibliography of the First Editions in Book Form of the Writings of James Russell Lowell* (New York, 1914), p. 77.

Biglow is that I am printing twelve copies on large paper of which you are down for one.

I enclose a copy of Sir Launfal for your wife. The cuts are horrible — but the print good.

always affectionately yours

J. R. L.

Elmwood: Monday [9 December? 1866]

Carissimo mio Ciarli,

I enclose a check for three tickets to the concerts. I hope to hear the next one.

The large-paper B. P.s are printing again & you will have one soon.

I am glad to see those John Bulls waking up at last to your scholarship. I hope they will pirate your Chaucer "Remarks" & put them in a handier shape.

affectionately yours always

J. R. L.

'The compact gold & violet brick of a book' in the letter by Child which follows is clearly the large-paper *Biglow, Second Series*, which Lowell inscribed to Child 27 May 1867. The description and time lapse fit perfectly, and further identification is afforded by Child's reference to 'Dosipeers,' the twelve paladins (Douzepers) of Charlemagne, corresponding to the twelve presumed recipients of the minute 'edition.' Finally, both Howells and Charles Godfrey Leland received the honorary degree of A.M. at the Harvard Commencement on 17 July 1867. In Elizabeth Robins Pennell's biography of Leland there is not only a letter from Lowell about the prospect of this award but an allusion to Child's invitation, which Leland could not accept, to come to his house at Commencement time.[16]

The first volume of *Bishop Percy's Folio Manuscript* was likewise issued in 1867. Child had been chiefly responsible for the final granting by the owners of permission to print (following at least two ineffectual efforts), and the published work was dedicated to him by the editors, J. W. Hales and F. J. Furnivall, in the following terms: 'Dedicated to Professor Francis James Child, of Harvard University, Massachusetts, U. S. at whose instigation, and to relieve English anti-

[16] Elizabeth R. Pennell, *Charles Godfrey Leland, a Biography* (Boston, 1905), I, 296.

17

quarians from whose reproaches (too well deserved,) this work was first undertaken.'

Sunday, 22 [i.e., 23] June. [1867]

My dear Friend,

The compact gold & violet brick of a book has been reproaching me all but a month for not sending thanks for it. I have been trusting to gay deceiving hopes of coming to Elmwood and talking over the book. But Lizzie had to take to her bed, the very day after it came, I think, and there she has remained, and I not far off. — You know very well how much I delight in the book & in having any book of yours straight from you: to be one of the Dosipeers who get between them the whole edition gratifies I know not what of the wicked Adam in my heart. I fear it will be a long while, more than one life-time, before I have anything of any sort to send back

Our representations in behalf of Howells & Leland are to be successful, judging from an inquiry of the President about middle names. Of course the secret is to be profoundly kept. I should ask Leland to come on & stay with me at Commencement time were Lizzie to be out of her bed. He will enjoy a compliment from Harvard very much and though I fancy he has to dig for a living could spare a few days. It will be pleasant to let the Philadelphians, whom he calls awfully slow, see that we know a man as far off as that.

I have got the first vol. of the Percy MS. Poor stuff most of it and in the main not new — but it's all genuine, bad or good, and answers my purpose. There is an appendix of "Loose Songs", of which the editors have made a very ostentatious concealment, which if it ever comes in your way I advise you to put up the chimney (where it will be in its element) or into the fire — where the authors no doubt are!! They are just as dirty as they can be, and I am glad that I am not particularly responsible for their coming out.

I hope to see you soon and to see Mrs. Lowell well. I feel much interest in your cabbages. You need to talk [?] to them to keep yourself practical enough for life — but what should I be if I *cultivated* that sort of thing?

Your loving

F. J. C.

[Attached is a clipping of a newspaper account of the robbery of a clergyman; to this Child has appended the word 'Wilbur?', no doubt alluding to the Reverend Homer Wilbur, 'editor' of *The Biglow Papers*.]

There follows a letter assigned tentatively to 1867 on the basis of the watermark. The scholar-friends at work.

Carissimo Ciarli!

I knew I should find it: eccolo quà! Knight's Tale "pitous & pitously".

> "Molt hautement i fist venir
> L'Ampereriz [et] l' Ampereres:
> Li *pitez* Rois, li *pitex* peres
> D'ax henorer fu molt engranz,
> Possessions lor dona granz."
>
> Barbazan & Méon i. 330.

You will readily see by the context that *pitex* must mean *pious* here. The King had come to honor the arrival of some *corsainz* at Soissons & the *ax* & *lor* refer to *them* not to *gent menue* just above.

Man of Law's Tale: such rhymes as "wound hid" were common (& not comic). Dante has a few. In the same poem — Barb. & Méon i. 274)

> "La Seinte Virge Leocade:
> En soupirant li dist, o, qu'a de
> Douceur" &c.

M. of L.'s Tale   "him & her."

> "Ne les loanges qu'à Diex [Deu] firent
> Et Cil et celes qui ce virent,"

i.e. both men & women. (Same page of B. & M.)

Now for "nailed."

> En son poig tint un fort espié quarrey
> à v clos d'or le confenon fermey
>   Girard of Viane 2164–5. (In Bekker's Fierabras).

It would seem here as if *fermey* were for *fermait* — but it probably is not.

> 2227   En son poig prist un roit espié forbi
>   À v clos d'or le confenon assis.

Unhappily the *fermey* & *assis* are rhymes
But, at any rate, here is a use for nails.
For the Maris astezer or *ateser* I guess Tyrwhitt may be right:

> O, Mars, O *atisour*, from *atiser*.

Mars presided over ovens, furnaces, &c from his fiery property.

affectionately always

J. R. L.

A mass by the young musician, John Knowles Paine, for many later years a distinguished professor of music at Harvard, was performed first in Berlin in 1867, and again in Boston in the spring of 1868. Child's endeavor to enlist support for the young Paine is typical of a life-long concern for promising scholars and artists. Equally typical is Lowell's ready response.

The opening lines of Child's letter suggest that it may have been written on Lowell's birthday, February 22. Communication on this day became traditional with Child as the years advanced.

[22 February? 1868]

My dear Boy,

You have had time to grow up since I saw you last, but you cant do it because you are a poet. I hear with grief that your wife has not been well. Please give her my love & sympathy. What I write for now is, to ask you if you dont want to encourage Paine to bring out his Mass — which he had performed in Berlin last winter with much success. We ought not to let so highminded & accomplished a fellow droop for want of appreciation at home. It may turn out that he has genius by and by — talent hat er ganz bedeutend.

If you will sign the paper I will send it to some music-mad people in Boston, & then to Paine and in two or three months I think the Mass will be forthcoming. I want Paine to make a little money by the performance, if possible, for he has spent two or three thousand dollars on this piece.

Ever your affectionate

Ciarli.

Elmwood, [February? 1868]

Caro mio,

I sign with both hands. Fanny sta meglio. You are a good boy to have thought of this for Paine & I hope it will come to something.

Ever your affectionate

J. R. L.

The 'Gower' in the next letter refers to Child's paper on the language of Gower's *Confessio Amantis*, delivered before the American Academy of Arts and Sciences 9 January 1866, and distributed privately, in preprint form, in the spring of 1868, after the fashion of the Chaucer paper of 1862. In the present case the pertinent volume of the *Memoirs* of the Academy did not appear until 1873.

Elmwood, 25th May. [1868]

Carissimo mio Ciarli!

I come on the wings of love tomorrow evening — & Fanny also if well enough.

Thank you a thousand times for the Gower. If I learn half as much from it as from the Chaucer, I shall be greatly indebted to you, as I am glad to be. But the two ought to be printed in a handy, & above all *accessible* volume, & I think we could find enough subscribers.

always affectionately yours

Lovelli.

Lowell's daughter Mabel (who became Mrs Edward Burnett in 1872) went abroad with Mr and Mrs James T. Fields in the spring of 1869. In view of this, and the mention of Saturday in conjunction with Lowell's birthday, the following letter may be dated with some confidence.

[20 February 1869]

Deliciae Meae,

Nothing shall keep me from the celebration of the ripening of your youth. Come of age you never will. When the other half of your adolescence shall have expired I shall give the party myself. It will be fun to see how your contemporaries have outgrown you. I note your advice about the donkey. That is not the key to which we will set our chant.

The other night I had some talk with Mabel at Miss Ashburner's — The freshest may she is I know of. I proposed to her to play some time in As You Like It, (she to be the heroine,) but I think I called Rosalind *Orlando!*

Tell her, if I did, that I never wanted to see her wrestling. I had forgotten that Rosalind had to appear in doublet & hose — which she thought an objection, of course. It was after she had gone away that it occurred to me I might have said *Orlando.*

I am sure that there is much in your lovely daughter that would come out in a good play, were she once launched. I should like to see her in Ion.

Ever your affectionate

Ciarli

Sat Morn

I hear that M. is going to Europe in April. How I wish you & Mrs. Lowell could take her. Impossible?

The efforts on behalf of Professor Corson suggested in the following letter seem to have born fruit with a swiftness unwonted in either academic or publishing circles, if Corson's *Handbook of Anglo-Saxon and Early English* (New York: Holt & Williams, 1871) is to be identified with the 'Dictionary of Old English.'

22 Oct. [1870?]

My dear James,

Do you object to saying a word or two in favor of that Dictionary of Old English by Prof Hiram Corson for which we have all subscribed? It hangs fire owing to the want of enterprise or means of Messrs Leypold & Holt. Corson wrote me last August that they proposed to get out one number, about a fifth of the whole, by the first of December, and asked me to write him a *recommend* & get some gentlemen of consequence to sign it. I have been guilty of the most shameful procrastination, a vice which I find by practice to be as bad as it is said to be in the copybooks. You think well of Corson, *I* think & have probably seen a specimen of the Dictionary. It is to be a regular thesaurus of old English within certain limits, and we have nothing of the kind.

Just send me then a few lines expressing (to Prof Hiram Corson) a desire that the work may go on & a conviction that it will be well received (if you have such a conviction, as I have) and you will perhaps help, certainly please, a very good scholar & worthy man.

Ever your loving friend
F Ciarli

I shall write a note myself, & get C. E. N. to do so.

Lowell's article on Chaucer, published in the July 1870 issue of the *North American Review* (ostensibly as a review of three recent books), was sent to Child for criticism before republication in Lowell's third volume of essays, *My Study Windows* (Boston, January 1871), which was dedicated to Child. An examination of the essay as republished shows that Lowell adopted certain of Child's suggestions while passing over others. Thus, the revision suggested for p. 158 has been carried out, the note about the non-Chaucerian poems has been altered, and a sentence has been added to render less dark the delicious fun about the security of women. On the other hand, the tribute to Child on p. 160 has not been modified, and the limiters remain unsocial. Most important, Child's strongly urged argument that Chaucer is after all a dramatic poet, in spite of Lowell's position to the contrary, has had no visible effect. And, finally, there is no mention of Ten Brink's book, suggested by Child in his footnote.

Dear Jamie

As I said the other night, your Chaucer article seems to me one of your best things. I have next to nothing to suggest, as you will see.

p. 158 I should revise the quotations by the Six Text. the 2d line of Fly from the press is better read in another copy Suffice *the thy* good.

p. 159 It was Bradshaw who suggested to *me* that those poems were not Chaucer's — (namely Court of Love, Cuckoo & Nightingale * Flour & Leaf,* Dream, Rom. of the Rose, Complaynt of Lover's Life, Praise of Women & half a dozen small pieces) *also doubted by Tyrwhitt
(You will of course, for the fact is not stated[?])
I wish you would *alter that note* & strike out on p. 160 "who has done more" &c. I am content to have "fittingly" remain if you think it should, but that is quite enough flattery for me.

182 — why call the limiters *unsocial*? (They go about in pairs until they have been 50 years under rule, & then they may walk alone, C. T. 7444) They seem to have been sociable to a fault. The delicious fun about the security of women where friars are thick is alluded to by you rather too darkly to be understood — is it not?

188–9. I still think you are too firm in your distinction The Sompnour's Tale, by omission of said lines[?], would it seems to me be to all intents & purposes a drama. Its characters are perfectly distinguished & *self*-distinguished. The lady speaks but four lines, but the lady comes out in her as plain as if she had been one of the chief characters. The imperent squier, the lord, & everybody, are not described but made to present themselves. Now whether the poet gets completely inside of a man & talks through his mouth — possesses him like the devil — or whether he makes himself the very man — it seems to me impossible to say & of no great matter. If Shakespeare had done the friar what difference would you have observed? I think that particular character as masterly as Falstaff and can see no difference in the way in which the two were created. C. & S. have also the same faults occasionally. C. makes the Pardoner talk of himself as only another person would & so does Shakspeare Richard III.

I have never seen anything to compare with your setting forth of the man Chaucer & you have left nothing for anybody else to add. How I wish I could have written it for a first lecture!

Your affectionate
Ciarli

You had better put in the title of Ten Brink's book & look the book over before you print.

In 1872 Lowell, 'grown learned (after a fashion) and dull,' as he put it,[17] from sixteen years of teaching, sought refreshment of spirit in extended travel abroad. Failing to secure a leave of absence, and provided with independent means through the sale of most of the Elmwood estate, he simply resigned his professorship (to take it up again, however, in 1874). The following note may reflect this radical step, though he did not sail for England (with Mrs Lowell) until July.

Elmwood, 23rd Jany, 1872.

Carissimo mio Ciarli,

I enclose my subscription to Chaucer's Society for the year, with best love to him & you, rejoicing to find that you have survived Mrs J. W. Howe. What geese they are with their Harvard College! I am just off for Boston with Mabel to have our photographs taken under supervision of Rowse.

affectionately always

J. R. L.

Writing from Berne in July 1873, Lowell, after referring specifically to his resignation, alludes to some difficulty, now obscure, regarding Child's own status. The 'fire' must be the great Boston Fire of November 1872. Lowell's visit to Oxford in June 1873 brought him his first honorary degree, when he became D.C.L. in the company of H. A. J. Munro, the editor of Lucretius, and John Tyndall, the physicist. The degree of LL.D. followed from Cambridge a year later, and three more LL.D.'s were acquired in 1884, as will appear below. Mountague Bernard, Lowell's host at All Souls, was Oxford's first Professor of International Law. This is not the only account of the visit to Oxford. With a special felicity it is described in a letter to Henry Adams bearing the outward semblance of prose but in reality a lively specimen of Lowell's ingenious rhyming.[18]

From this time on for several years, and particularly during Lowell's sojourns abroad, balladry plays a conspicuous role in the correspondence. Child by now, and partly under the stimulus of Gruntvig's

[17] In a letter to Jane Norton, 17 February 1872 (*Letters of James Russell Lowell*, II, 282).
[18] See *New Letters of James Russell Lowell*, pp. 198–201.

24

interest and encouragement, was fairly embarked upon the detailed prosecution of his great work. Actually, at the moment Lowell wrote, Child was abroad himself, having been suddenly dispatched to England by Mrs Child for his health's sake. He was gone eight weeks, and made another trip abroad in the summer of 1874.

The 'grandson' referred to at the end of the letter is Mabel Lowell Burnett's first child, James Lowell Burnett (later James Burnett Lowell), born 4 February 1873.

Hôtel du Faucon,
Berne, 29th July, 1873.

My dear Friend,

your letter came to me here last evening & was a great pleasure, I need not say. We have been in Switzerland for something over a week enjoying it after the manner of grandparents, & climbing the mountains with our opera-glass. I am heartily weary of perigrination [sic], but Fanny enjoys everything so freshly & sweetly that it keeps me up. We have had no adventures — not so much as the loss of a kerchief — till a hurricane leapt down on us the other day as we were going up the lake of the four Cantons. Mt Pilatus did himself credit — for a stiffer blow I never saw while it lasted. Fanny was sent below, but I staid on deck & was wet through in less than a minute though under an awning. It struck us as suddenly as a shot. I dried off afterwards in a thorough draught & caught no cold — which was pretty well at fifty four!

I am very glad to hear you are at work on the ballads & wish I were by to collogue — advice I shouldn't venture. But I shall be at home again before you are *fertig*. I don't think anything will persuade me to don my ball & chain again. I didn't resign in a huff but deliberately, though their stopping my salary gave me a good occasion. I think it would have been handsomer to have continued half of it after sixteen years service the latter part of [it] against my will. However, I wasn't in the least cross about it, nor am now, & I must have given it up after the fire at any rate. I had a very pleasant time at Oxford. I was the guest of Mountague Bernard at All Souls, & dined at Corpus with the Dons on Gaudy Day. There's a college for you. Why, the rogues have a *cordon bleu* in their kitchen & instead of our funeral bakemeats we had a dinner that would not have shamed Vifour. I wish you could have seen me in my scarlet gown, balancing my too-small cap with anxious care & humming to myself "some in rags & some in tags & some in a velvet gown!" I am sure you would have laughed despite the august nature of the event. What especially pleased me was to go up with two men like Munro & Tyndall instead of the generals & things. I hope you take too desponding a view of the College (as I am sure you take a too favorable of my value to it) — though

I think the Overseers behaved like a board of Brokers about you. All that, I trust, is well over & not likely to come up again. I hope to address you as Professor so long as we both shall live. Tell Miss Sedgwick that I half wrote a letter to her last winter on hearing she was not so well as usual — but learning that she was better bethought me that I had no business to be writing to such charming young ladies & suppressed it. We are going down into Italy from here & shall probably winter in Rome. Then Northward again & if there be time we shall run over Norway. But I shall be at home next summer, Godwilling. I am like a barnacle who has mistaken a ship's bottom for a rock. Give both our loves to Mrs Child & to the Nortons when you see them. *They* have seen the Grandson!

Goodbye,
always affectionately your
J. R. L.

There follow two notes from Lowell, now back in academic harness. In the first we see him again undertaking a bit of investigation on Child's behalf.

In 1876 a separate Professorship of English was finally established at Harvard, and Child became its first incumbent. Thus freed, after twenty-five years, from the reading of themes, he was thenceforth able to concentrate more intensively upon his ballad work.

Elmwood, 19th Oct^r, 1875.

Carissimo mio Ciarli,

    it is in the vith Tome of P. P. & not the fifth.

"Folio 115. De quodam Judaeo qui imaginem in vadimonium recepit." *Voilà tout.* It occurs in Gautier de Coinsy col. 543. "Du Juif qui prist en gage l'ymage Nostre Dame." It is a long & marvellous tale but without the comic touch of which you spoke. The merchant does not pledge an image (as the title would lead one to think) but takes an image in a church to witness.

tout à toi
J. R. L.

Elmwood, 19th July, 1876.

It was very good of you to think of me, *carissimo mio Ciarli*, but I can't afford any more books just now than what I have already ordered. I should have come to answer in person but for the *gran caldo*.

I found it pleasant to read an article of Newcomb's in the last N.A.R. on the likelihood of the sun's giving-out in caloric. He squanders it so, that I think it probable. That & the flies! I have no doubt Homer had

26

knocked his own nose sideways often enough before he called the little fiends untameable.[19]

affectionately yours always

J. R. L.

Early in 1877 Child and Lowell were fellow lecturers at the newly founded Johns Hopkins University, drawn thither by the discerning and persuasive President Gilman. The friendship, already firmly established, perceptibly deepened during these weeks of intimate contact, at the same time that the special abilities and achievements of each received mutual recognition in unstinting measure. Thus Lowell wrote to Charles Eliot Norton:

This gave Child a chance to speak of . . . , which he did as excellently well as he lectures on Chaucer and reads him, and that is saying a great deal. You lost, by the way, a very great pleasure in not hearing him read the Nonnes Prestes tale. I certainly never heard anything better. He wound into the meaning of it (as Dr. Johnson says of Burke) like a serpent, or perhaps I should come nearer to it if I said that he injected the veins of the poem with his own sympathetic humor till it seemed to live again. I could see his hearers take the fun before it came, their faces lighting with the reflection of his. I never saw anything better done. I wish I could inspire myself with his example, but I continue dejected and lumpish. . . .

Child goes on winning all ears and hearts. I am rejoiced to have this chance of seeing so much of him, for though I loved him before, I did not know *how* lovable he was till this intimacy.[20]

And again to Jane Norton, in describing the Johns Hopkins Commemoration, with addresses by Professors Silvester and Gildersleeve, among others:

Silvester paid a charming compliment to Child, and so did Gildersleeve. The former said that he (C.) had invented a new pleasure for them in his reading of Chaucer, and G., that you almost saw the dimple of Chaucer's own smile as his reading felt out the humor of the verse. The house responded cordially. If I had much vanity I should be awfully cross, but I am happy to say that I have enjoyed dear Child's four weeks' triumph (of which he alone is unconscious) to the last laurel-leaf. He is *such* a delightful creature. I never saw so much of him before, and should be glad I came here if it were for [nothing but] my nearer knowledge and enjoyment of *him*.[21]

[19] *Iliad*, XVII, 570.
[20] Baltimore, 18 February 1877 (*Letters of James Russell Lowell*, III, 10).
[21] 'Bahltimer,' 22 February 1877 (*Letters of James Russell Lowell*, III, 11–12).

27

Similarly Child:

J. L.'s good looks and insinuating ways carry off the palm entirely from my genius and learning, but then I am as much fascinated as anybody, and don't mind.[22]

Not long after the conclusion of the Johns Hopkins series, Lowell, intimating that he *should* like to see a play of Calderón,[23] accepted an appointment by President Hayes as United States Minister to Spain. He set sail from Boston 14 July 1877, much annoyed at the accompanying fanfare. Child's account of the circumstances, written to Norton, is quoted herewith. (John Holmes, retiring and much loved younger brother of the Autocrat of the Breakfast Table, appears more than once in the Child-Lowell correspondence.)

I saw Lowell yesterday and said goodbye. He more than half repents accepting his appointment. His wife was down with rheumatism. There is something in the air for I am struck with gout — very mildly. I am to go to Newcastle for the day tomorrow if I can go without hobbling. — Poor Jacobus was made quite wretched by Alexander, the Cunard man's getting up an escort for him to the outer light. The revenue cutter Gallatin & the steam tender Hamblin (ought an ambassador to have anything to do with such political craft?) will convey the friends of the Hon. James Russell Lowell from Long Wharf to the stream, where they will take the Parthia. If Lizzie & the children were here, I should accept Alexander's invitation (which included the members of your family — but I dare say your invitation has been forwarded to you & you know all about the matter) I should take Helen & Sue & let them see an ocean steamer. Provided that I had not arthritis. — Of course the custom-house will be well represented. Simmons will make L. a speech. "Josiah Quincy is going, a man that I never would let speak at Commencement dinners"! Mary & Julia Felton, & Ned Holmes & his wife are the only fellow passengers I know of. If life were longer, and I were richer, I should wish to go over with J. R. John Holmes has as good as promised to pay him a visit in Spain. John goes down tomorrow & I shall pay *him* a visit to learn how things went off.[24]

The two notes next printed below are Lowell's farewells to Child. *Romania*, mentioned in the second note, and reappearing later in the correspondence, had been founded in 1872 by Paul Meyer and Gaston Paris as a 'revue trimestriel consacré à l'étude des langues et des littéra-

[22] Quoted in H. E. Scudder, *James Russell Lowell, a Biography* (Cambridge, Mass., 1901), II, 214.

[23] W. D. Howells, *My Literary Friends and Acquaintance* (New York, 1900), p. 238.

[24] Letter of 13 July 1877, in the Norton papers, Harvard Library.

tures romanes.' It may be noted that Lowell's set of the early volumes came eventually to the Lowell Memorial Library at Harvard.

Elmwood, 10th July, 1877.

Dear old Ciarli,

I enclose the German bookseller's bill which you were so good as to say you would see to. Not "see to" in the sense which I believe is that of kite-fliers on the Exchange, for I have money in the Bank & have asked Mr Snow to honour your cheque whenever it comes. If you don't come to see us before we go! — why, I at least shall come to see you. O how bothered & tired I am! but I have paid all my debts but about thirty dollars, have bought a letter of credit for £500. & paid in the money (where it came from I still marvel), got an *Eco de Madrid* for ease in talking to the King, & am ready for my *nunc dimittis!*

always your affectionate

J. R. L.

Elmwood, Friday night. [13 July 1877]

God bless you, dear Ciarli, for your loving words every one of which I echo from my inner heart.

The *Romania* comes by post, & when I get to Paris, I will see about it. No number is due now for three months.

You must write to me now & then — won't you?

à dios mil veces!

J. R. L.

Care of Department of State, Washington.

The shadow overhanging the next letter is the death of Jane Norton, which actually had occurred in May 1877, before Lowell's departure for Spain. This loss brought a sorrow to both Lowell and Child which tinged the rest of their lives. Her younger sister Grace, as well as the brother Charles, remained as close links between the two friends.

Child is also plainly cast down at the thought of a repetition of the Johns Hopkins course without the companionship of Lowell, whose Palm Sunday letter next following comes as a tardy and faraway but none the less plangent echo.

Thomas Donaldson, Harvard '34, lawyer and leading citizen of Baltimore, died 4 October 1877, leaving nine children. Tom Sayers, Champion of England, had been dead for twelve years, but his fame persisted. The marriage alluded to is that of Sara Sedgwick, a younger sister of Mrs Charles Eliot Norton, to William Darwin, son of the naturalist. Justin Winsor succeeded John Langdon Sibley as Librarian of Harvard College in the autumn of 1877, after nine years as Librarian of the Boston Public Library. Ephraim W. Gurney was Professor of History at Harvard for many years.

To the
> *Hon. James Russell Lowell, Madrid.*

Christmas, 1877.

My dear Jamie,

I never meant not to write to you, but only to wait till a molle tempus came. Perhaps I had better wait till March still, for the nearer the day comes for me to go to Baltimore, without you, the more repulsive is the thought. Not only shall I be missing you, but the troubles that have come to the Gilmans will make it impossible for one to be at ease with them. There is one more change there. Mr[?] Tom Donaldson is dead, and has left an all but desperate burden for his wife & children — two insane sons, whose support devours 2/3 of their income.

I slave at lectures day & night, but mostly night. Last summer's operations on my house left me more tired than I ever was in my life, and when this term began, I felt as little like coming up to time as if I had had a round with Tom Sayers. But what a tonic the cold air is! In a couple of weeks I was comfortable enough in my college harness, although the extra treat appointed for February cowed me a good deal. Then came Sara's marriage. I could not muster a hearty feeling to write her a letter with, though there are few people of whom I have been more fond. I did not know myself — and to write such a letter as I finally did 'twere best not know myself. But Christmas will thaw a fellow's heart as long as there is one drop unfrozen, and today I have written as I ought to have done before, though I was near being spoiled for it by thinking of Jane and writing a few unhappy lines to Grace. She is firmer, less thunder struck, confounded. When I think of what has gone from us, and so suddenly, for I took no warning from Jane's face, trusting always to her promise that she would get well, I wonder that I can occupy myself with what is left, even in the halfhearted way in which I do. My foot used to feel so firm on the earth; now I should not be surprised to see the heavens roll up as a scroll and the hollow crust we walk on vanish into thin air the next minute. — However, thinking of you & looking round at my books and away from Shady Hill to the willows along the east, which have almost a spring yellow in their spray — for we have no frost this extraordinary December — makes the world seem a little more real. I believe it may last till you come home. —

And so you are really writing letters and holding conferences about 50 cts more or less on tonnage! It makes me mad to think of it. If I loved the country better I should submit to your being engaged in the business of keeping up its respectability, with less impatience: but my dear Jamie, the scapegraces at Washington are disgracing us faster than even you can clean us up. Non ragionam di lor. — Do you see any Catalans? Is there a good Catalan-Spanish dictionary, and how do they pronounce Briz? I wish I knew enough not to miscall their writers at least. We are receiving a lot of Catalan things (Milás & others) just now, but no ballads. Milás ballads are so good that your excellency ought to urge him, Briz, or any such, to sweep the province.

Kristensen, the Jute, has collected in a very few years more than a couple of hundred ballads, mostly in a small district of Jutland, many of which were not known before. It is an everlasting cause of grief that this had not been timely done in England. I have had an Aberdeen man, rather his wife, noting down what can now be collected in Old Deir, and such trash as I get! Better work the mines[?] of Spain & Denmark. À propos, Kinloch's manuscripts, that I had such trouble with, have just been sold, in Edinburgh. The one I offered £12 for sold for £30. It was not worth £12 to anybody but me. It is my hope that some public library bought it: then I will have it copied for two or three pound and shame the man that charged me 50 guineas. It seemed as if the demon had entered into copyists. I wrote to Champion in Paris to have a transcript made of 6 vols of chansons pop., those collected under the Fortoul commission, and the man informed me that he had had *one* done at about 1500 francs, and that the whole would cost from 5 to 6 thousand. I wrote him a most polite but decided letter, and yesterday he says that all 6 are done, & much cheaper. If not, we shall want the new bequest of 20000 dollars to pay for them. —

I am inclined to think that Winsor will be an acquisition for us. The future of the Boston Library is so uncertain that they say two or three people have revoked bequests since Winsor left it and have turned them our way. — I saw John Holmes on Election Day. He was well enough, but did not seem to me to feel sufficient enterprise to come out to you. That will be a disappointment. The Gurneys I suppose you did not expect to retain. Perhaps it would be better for you to see nothing but Spain while you are there — and perhaps you will come home the sooner if you don't. When I heard (through your last letter to Grace N.) what you had to do, with your Yankee secretary to shoulder as well as your proper business, I exclaimed. The gout, we may hope, will henceforth lette you nothing for to daunce: [25] but you will have a cold winter and a blazing hot summer, an ignorant ungrateful and pickpocket government to stand up for, no time for reading, or for versing, formal dinners, eternal white chokers, no lounging along the Charles River or strolling up towards

[25] Cf. 'The Nun's Priest's Tale,' *Canterbury Tales*, VII, 2840.

Waltham Jesu Maria! But all my thoughts are black, Christmas though it be. Life is so very short and the world has been so dear. Sometimes when I detect the green coming back to the grass, I feel as if something might be left. Gracious goodness is this after all an incubus of lectures? Shall I see straight again in March? I don't know, but for the present I cannot see otherwise. — I shall write [if?] possible from Baltimore and tell you of your (Julia) Valentines. Shall I have to dine with those paddies again, think you? And what shall I say to the lady who gave you (and me) the Life of Edgar Poe. Pooh, pooh? Love and ever so much sympathy to the ambassadress.

Always your excellencys fondest slave,
Ciarli

In Lowell's Palm Sunday letter the 'little Greek book in Mr Sibley's showcase' may be identified with a manuscript of Hippocrates' *Aphorisms* executed in type facsimile by the Reverend John Thomasine in England in 1733. The penmanship is of remarkable quality, and the volume, in a handsome contemporary inlaid binding, shows evidence of having been on exhibition for a long period. Librarian Sibley's showcase or 'Closet' was the parent and grand-parent of the Widener Treasure Room and the Houghton Library respectively.

Legacion de los Estados Unidos   14th April, 1878
    de America en España   Palm Sunday.

Particular

Dear Ciarli,

I have noticed that Class & Phi Beta poems almost always begin with an "as" — at any rate they used to in my time before a certain Boylston Professor took 'em in hand. E.g.

> As the last splendors of expiring day
> Round Stoughton's chimneys cast a lingering ray,
> So —

And sometimes there was a whole flight of *as*-es leading up to the landing of a final *so* where one could take breath & reflect on what he had gone through. Now you will be sure that I didn't mean to begin my letter thus, but it was put into my head by the earthquake you have been making in Baltimore, the wave from which rolled all the way across the ocean &

splashed audibly on these distant shores, & as all my associations are with dear Old Cambridge, why, naturally I found myself murmuring —

> As when the Earthquake stomps his angry foot
> A thousand leagues the frightened billows scoot,
> So when my Ciarli &c.

I was delighted to hear of it, though it was just what I expected, for didn't my little bark attendant sail more than a year ago? It gave me a touch of homesickness too, for I look back on that month as one of the pleasantest of my life & here I am not as who should say altogether & precisely happy. Yet I hope to get something out of it that will tell bye & bye. The ceremonial, of which there is plenty, of course is naught, & I make acquaintance so slowly that I hardly know anybody (except officially) even yet, but I have at last got hold of an intelligent bookseller & am beginning to get a few books about me. I call him intelligent & so he is — but he knows nothing about books except their price & that is the case with all of them here. His merit is that he will try to get a book for you if you ask him & that is *not* the case with all of 'em by a long chalk. It is a queer place. There are no sales of books here as everywhere else, but when anybody dies who had a library, a bookseller is sent for who appraises it *en bloc* — then, if you are able to get access to the books, you find the widow ignorant of the value of any particular volume you want & therefore suspicious & reluctant to sell it all. Moreover, as the expert is paid by a per-centage on the valuation — don't you see? This Gayangos told me the other day. *He* has some exquisite old books, by the way — a Góngora among others that would have tempted me to ruin had it been for sale. It is a manuscript on vellum made as a present to the Conde-duque de Olivares when he was in the flush of his *privanza*. Each poem is dated on the margin, & in the index the copyist marks certain ones as falsely attributed to Góngora & says the poet told him so himself. It is exquisitely done like that little Greek book in Mr Sibley's showcase — Anacreon isn't it?

I have just succeeded in getting a copy of the series printed for the *Bibliofilos Españoles* which is very hard to come at & cost me $105 in paper. It contains one or two things worth having — but I bought mainly with a view to the College Library one of these days. I have also bought the photolithographic of Cuesta's *editio princeps* of D. Q. for the sake of Hartzenbusch's notes, which, by the way, show a singular dulness of perception & *correct* Cervantes in a way that makes me swear. But they are worth having as showing the emendations that have been made or proposed, the *when* & *by whom*. I have, too, the Burgos 1593 *Crónica* of the Cid a very fair copy & Damas-Hinard's edition of the *poem*. My bookseller whose name is Junquera (Calle Salud, 14) is to get me a list of Catalan books, that is, of reprints or first publication of Mss. There is a dictionary now publishing in parts — but I wait for its completion & of course Junquera can't tell me whether it is well done or not. I bought a

33

little *á mano* one which I bought for you & shall send by post with this, though with some doubt of its ever arriving. It may be better than nothing, but when I looked for your word *Briz* in it I found it not. I am told to pronounce it as in Spanish the *th* as in *frith*. But your Ms. is so delightfully inscrutable that I am not sure but I have *made* a word out of it wholly unlike the one you meant.

I fear what you say of my being thrown away here may turn out true. There is a great deal to do & of a kind for which I cannot get up a very sincere interest, claims & customs duties & even, God save the mark, Brandreth's pills! I try to do my duty but feel sorely the responsibility to people three thousand miles away who know not Joseph & probably think him unpractical. I remember how you felt & I felt when the Overseers were discussing you & my cheeks burn all of a sudden. You would laugh if you knew how my fear of not doing just as I should kept me awake for the first three or four months & contributed I think to my gout of which I have had three fits since I came the last so bad that Fanny sent for a doctor. But I am all right now & am getting over my damned *mauvaise honte* in speaking Spanish & French. I have lost all my Italian oddly enough. When I first got here I kept mixing it with Spanish & now *that* has crowded it all out, so that I have to think five minutes to recall the forms of a verb.

We are going off day after tomorrow on our furlough & our plan is to take a steamer & get as far as Athens, perhaps Stamboul, if there is no war. We have seen Seville, Córdoba, Granada & Toledo each excellent in itself & Toledo queer even after Italy & Sicily. But the *shrinkage* is frightful — Toledo especially is full of ruin & what is worse of indifference to ruin. Yet there is something oriental in my own nature which sympathizes with this "let her slide" temper of the *hidalgos*. They go through all the forms of business as they do of religion without any reference to the thing itself just as they offer you their house (dating their notes to you *de su casa*) & everything in it. But they are very friendly & willing to be helpful where they can. I love the jauds for a' that. They are unenterprising & unchangeable. The latest accounts of them are just like the earliest, & they have a firm faith in Dr Mañana — he will cure everything or if he can't it doesn't signify. In short there is a flavor of Old Cambridge about 'em as O. C. used to be when I was young & the world worth having. Since what happened last year at Shady Hill & what is likely to happen now — *paciencia y barajar*, to be sure, but I don't like new partners & the game isn't worth playing. I am glad & sorry to be away. Goodbye, dear old fellow,

Your affectionate

J. R. L.

Pongami ruegole à ll pp de su Señora. By the way they all pronounce it siñora like the Italians which puzzles one.

In the next letter Child alludes to the death of Queen María de las Mercedes, first wife of Alfonso XII, which occurred 26 June 1878, just two days after her eighteenth birthday and five months after her wedding. The same virulent form of typhus which caused her death was to strike down Mrs Lowell a year later. The Queen's fate moved Lowell to a sonnet which was included in *Heartsease and Rue* (1888).

The visit of William James to Baltimore early in 1878, also alluded to, may well have been the occasion of the caricatures of Child by James shown in Plate VI. These caricatures have been reproduced from the originals among the James Papers in the Harvard College Library.

George Martin Lane, Child's classmate, and Professor of Latin at Harvard 1851–94, was the author not only of *Latin Pronunciation* (1871), which brought about the abandonment in America of the traditional 'English' pronunciation, but also of 'The Lay of the Lone Fishball,' whence arose *Il Pesceballo*. His second wife was Mrs Fanny Bradford Clark. Charles R. Lanman, the 'promising Indian scholar,' left Johns Hopkins for Harvard in 1880, to serve as Professor of Sanskrit for half a century.

Cambridge, Aug. 12. [1878]

Dear Jamie,

I never could have believed that I could let you represent me and my government (ego et rex meus) for thirteen months, through heat & cold, marriage & funeral, and I write to you but once. It is because I have been in a state of spirits too feeble to do anything but the day's work. No matter. The streem of life now droppeth on the chymbe.[26] I hope it is only because it is bunged up: and that a few weeks away from here will clear away the obstruction for a time. And O if Esop's old woman might only say over the empty tun, what good wine was once herein! But she will not. It was the 14 April that you wrote, and I heard that you were actually on your way to Greece from C. E. N. I hope you brought much back and one day will whisper whence you stole those balmy spoils. Did the παῖδες τῶν Ἑλλήνων make restitution of the flasks of wine which Stillman sent you, and pirates drank? Were you caught by the University of Athens, and made to stand a eulogy or a dithyrambic ode? I wonder. All these questions you will answer some day — ὁ θεὸς μα δώσῃ! — either here in my room, smoking your καπνουκυλινδρον — or in your own study, drinking your pipe. But wo for your summer! Is not an ambassador's

---

[26] 'The Reeve's Prologue,' *Canterbury Tales*, I, 3894–3895:

Til that almost al empty is the tonne.
The streem of lyf now droppeth on the chymbe.

35

togary[?] hotter than a professor's gown? and what do you do when you melt? I do not know whether the death of the good little queen (Heaven rest her soul!) aggravated or lightened your ceremony. I suppose on the whole you have more quiet during mournings than during festivals. Any way the first month of your second year is gone, and you are to be away but eleven months more. I have sworn it, and oaths must have their course, you know. I could almost strike hands with the collector of the port, port-master Tobey and the mayor of Boston to give the Hon. J. R. L. an ovation when he comes back. Returning is by no means as tedious as go o'er, and I could cheer you into port though I had no heart to cheer you out. —

Now I have nothing to tell you of myself more than that I miss you con-sumedly. And didn't I miss you in Baltimore! Julia Valentine could not stand your absence. She went off to England a week after my arrival, to marry one of her Thomas nephews to an English girl. Ere this her sugar shovel bonnet may have been inquiring for you at your excellency's palace. I worked all the time in Baltimore from 9 to 6, at the university, where I had a room, and needed one, for my books. The people got more ballads than they wanted in the course of 20 lectures, I am sure. Sometimes I spent a whole hour in following out the history & forms of one ballad. That was to make my hour heavy and academical. Then I put two pretty ballads into an hour, with lots of Italian, Spanish, Danish or Swedish translations, to make my hour light and not discourage the numerous ladies. One rainy day I did not draw a crowd. That was because you were not to come after me. Besides my regular 20, which might as well have been 12, I explained Hamlet to 'em in ten hours, at 12 o'clock. This cost me no trouble and the Shaksperian hour was, I am sure, more relished than the other. I told Gilman — who always warns the audience that the lectures are "academic", but who wants his public entertained — that I did not think the two went well together — that I had rather do one or the other, a public or a university lecture. He very cordially assented, and put me down in his advertisement for 79 for both! and a play of Shakspere besides. All that I cannot do. I am main weary and do not pick up. What to do next year I know not. I keep clear of Shakspere for more reasons than one, but one of the reasons is because I consider your course as promised for the year 80. Were it not for the pay — small as it is — I should certainly stop after the third course. I *must* earn 8 or 10 hundred extra for the present: but the consequences are bad — nothing else done and no real vacation. Meanwhile I have been offered 750 for *three* lectures in N. York, but could not accept the opportunity because of the previous engagement to do 20 for 850 net. —

I went this year to the house of a Mrs. Egerton where I lived with several nice young fellows belonging to Johns Hopkins, one of whom Lanman (he gave a lecture on the discoveries at Olympia while we were at B.) is a most promising Indian scholar, and such a good boy! He has made me a short visit since February. — Gilman has a most charming wife, who was so

36

kind and sweet to me that I am bound to love her always. Everybody inquired after you of course. Mr Garrett did not think it worth while to give a reception for *me* alone. I begged off from any attention from him except seeing his Arab horses, and one Sunday he took me to Montebello — four miles — where he has a thousand acres mostly devoted to stock and especially horses. I saw such beauties! Reverdy J.[ohnson] came to see me often, but the last hour of the night was not spent with him as in 77. Henry Johnston and Harriet Lane wished to give me "a swell dinner or a swell reception" — and ask *all* the nice people: but I entreated that I might exchange for a Sunday dinner with nobody and they goodnaturedly allowed me to have my choice — I did *not* see Miss Poulaine. Miss Make-peace I must not forget. She passed the winter in Boston and I saw her often. She spent a week with us too. —

I had Wm James with me for a fortnight in Baltimore. He gave ten lectures on the Brain as the organ of the mind and made a decided impression. I heard the last, in which he offered some reasons for not accepting the theory that we are automatons unreservedly. At that lecture your friend Mrs Thomas & her daughter, and Miss Bessie King, whom you did not see I think — a sweet little demi-quakeress that is fond of Greek & pictures — wears a grey dress and a peachy cheek — not the girl to be explained as an automaton. Mrs. Thomas was delighted with the lecture. She enjoyed being explained as a machine, she said, — *when you know just how it is.* — Wm J. was sleepless & restless, and as it turned out, not because the lectures troubled him, but because his fate was in the scales and Miss Alice Gibbons would not say the word he wanted But she did in June and in July they were married, and now they are happy together at the Adirondack mountains. She serves as eyes to him, and as she has a sweet low voice truth comes mended from her lips.[27] Wm has already begun a manual of Psychology — in the honeymoon — but then they are both writing it. — Lane has married too, with the same suddenness — Mrs. Clark. —

Your Catalan dictionary came with your letter, bon Jaume, thank you much. It answers all my purposes. I wish I could go down to Barcelona (up for you) and get somebody to teach me how to read. Milàs Catalan ballads are about the best of all for color and music. But I do not look at ballads now, or hardly: there is always something else to be done. I keep an eye on all the books I think you would like, and as we can spend nigh 16000 a year now, one gets pretty much what he asks for. I am even proposing to the Council to buy 3500 dollars worth of Medlicott's books — including some really fine things in the way of old authors More, Erasmus, Spenser, Froissart etc. We surely ought to have first editions of all the poets, of all the great literary pieces since printing began. Our former poverty has made even the Council timid about buying rare books. If we

[27] Pope, *Eloisa to Abelard*, l. 66:
    And truths divine came mended from that tongue.

dont we shall have to spend our money on a huge quantity of recent things which will be forgotten in twenty years. — We are building a big gymnasium between the Scientific School & J. Holmes's house, and a big hall for lectures and lessons back of the site of Lane's house. You can have the luxury of a private room attached to your lecture room. They are beginning to pet us Jamie — just as we are leaving them. But I take the word back — the word leave. You are good for more than a score yet.

"What was likely to happen" when you wrote did not happen. Mrs. Norton seems to be very well, saving her power of speech. Grace lives by miracle. She certainly will sink under her cares & sorrows, I often fear — and just now she seems to be less bright than ever. For Jane, that is gone, and taken so much of the world with her, if she has really died, it matters not exactly how much dust & misery is left: but I am happy to believe that you know she is & was deathless. Don't let poets falter, or where shall we be! Though I don't value the philosophers over much, their talk frightens me like ghost stories. When I go back to the poets I see how I have been fooled.

Love to Mrs. Lowell. I hope she gets some enjoyment besides the happiness of being with you. I love you always with my heart dear Jamie.

Ciarli.

I see John Holmes sometimes. He will not come to you: so come to him.

Late in June 1879 Mrs Lowell fell ill of the same virulent form of typhus of which Queen Mercedes had died only the year before. Her life was more than once despaired of, there were frequent relapses, and she never really recovered her health, remaining in a semi-invalid state until her death in England in 1885. The crisis of her illness and her continuing ill health darken the letters immediately following with a gloom only thickened by the death of Mrs Andrews Norton in September 1879 and resultant anxiety over her daughter Grace, who had borne the chief stress both of Jane's earlier death and her mother's long decline.

Lowell's secretary, Dwight Reed, had proved of invaluable assistance during the acute stage of Mrs Lowell's illness. Without him, Lowell said, 'I should have gone quite desperate.' [28]

Scarboro Beach:
July 28, 79

My dear Jamie,

I have not written to you for so long because I would not repeat my last doleful letter. I was purposing to make amends by something more cheer-

[28] Quoted in Scudder, *James Russell Lowell*, II, 251.

ful, when the news came that made all your friends hold their breath. Grace Norton gave some relief at last, derived from a letter of yours to Mabel, and today she writes of a letter from Field which seems to warrant a belief that danger is over, while it reveals an extremity that even the one dreadful line of the telegraph did not express. How glad we are it is no need today[?] to say. Even the losing of your promised visit seems nothing now. But soon we shall recur to that disappointment. I had begun to wish it more than all for Grace's sake: for she had been so depressed that I could think of nothing besides that might rouse her, and I could see that the hope of seeing you did have an animating power: and though she had always argued against my unqualified (and "unsanctified") vows for your throwing up your ministry and apostleship in Spain and coming to these Indies, where surely there is *no wale* [29] of such ministers as you, she was secretly more than content that you should come home for a visit. There seems to be small hope for anything good to her as far as we can now see. It is not merely that her mother's state is very sad and saddening, and that the care Grace has to bear is enough to exhaust twice anybody's strength, or anybody's but such a woman's; that is not the worst: the decay of Mrs N's faculties suggests awful fears to G. of what may be the fate of all that has looked least mortal. You will guess what I mean. Love is the thing she needs: your letters, I am sure, have been one of her chief stays, perhaps the best of all. She may read hope in or through your eyes when she cant see it herself, poor dear angel in the dark that she is — for nothing can begin to intimate the goodness there has been in Grace. I think she has surpassed anything I have ever witnessed in courage and self command. —

If the consequences of this sickness do not prove bad, and the recovery is as complete and speedy as I have known in other cases, perhaps you may yet come. The old saying of Dr Jackson that no typhoid fever is too severe to forbid hope, and none so slight as not to justify apprehension seems to have been strongly confirmed in the first half, and the second we will willingly take for granted. This sickness is but too strong a confirmation also of the danger of having friends out of sight for four years. When you spoke of two only, that time seemed to include much that was threatening. I have heard somebody say that Mrs. Lowell liked the life in Spain, and that alone enabled me to see how you should stay on. I am very glad she has liked her life there, and wish there may be much more pleasure in store for her. The second two years must naturally be far pleasanter than the others, since you know all the ropes. (How *do* they walk Spanish really? Don't forget the step: I have never seen it figured save in Peter Parley.) The fandango and the bolero are I suppose not de rigueur for ambassadors, but are you not expected to do a minuet of

[29] Apparently an allusion to a story given by Robert Pearse Gillies in *Memoirs of a Literary Veteran* (London, 1851), I, 18; cf. Child's letter of 22 February 1880, where the story is specifically mentioned.

the court on high days, such as I have seen at theatres? I have heard a whisper that the king said — Mr Lowell — who has taught us something about our own language. The remark gives me confidence in the stability of the Spanish monarchy — so judicious a prince! It is but one of a hundred that we should be happy to hear. If you would tell us the name of the proper court journal we would subscribe and save your modesty: for else some day you will have to tell one or two of us some of these things, to excuse your staying. — I am reading Don Quixote now to the girls and they are enjoying it as I wanted my offspring to do. It never was half so delightful before: and what must it be to him that knows Spain & the Spaniards well, though of course all the world can get at the kernel.

My dear Jamie, when you give my love to your wife, tell her that I send it trembling, feeling what the difference might have been, and join my wife's to mine. There are many things that I should like to say to you and ask you about, but not now. Heaven keep you and yours safe the rest of the time.

Your loving Ciarli.

4 vols, I think, of the French Texts have come for you: *only* 4. It looked as if there should have been more. Your Romania comes like a letter from you.

Sunday, Sept. 28, 1879.

My dear Jamie,

I never thought that I was one of the people who are quite sure that *now* all their friends troubles are over, and yet I can't deny that I leapt much too suddenly to that conclusion in your case. Had *I* not had a typhoid fever? Your case was to be sure very much worse than mine, and apparently it is much worse than any I ever heard of before. Now I wish most of all that I could have been with you all the time. Your lonesomeness, with nobody but your secretary, is harrowing to think of, even now, when according to distant reports of your letters, and a nearer one through Field to Grace N., you seem to have been rejuvenated through your joy at the progress of the recovery. G. N. has sent or given me all her news about you, and her mother's sickness, though more and more distressing, never either put you out of her mind or qualified the intense distress she had about you. I know that she has written to you of her mother's death: she told me so. She feels a peace, of more than one description, now: but whether she will not soon feel the care that is "loss of care by old care done" [30] remains to be seen. Many daughters have done gloriously, but she

---

[30] *Richard II*, IV, i, 196–197:
> My care is loss of care, by old care done;
> Your care is gain of care, by new care won.

has excelled them all. It is 21 months since the beginning of this end: and think how close it followed upon that May which took away our dearest flower! More than three years Grace has been subjected to a dreadful strain, and nobody has been more astonished at her strength than she. She was at her post day & night, and no relieving guard, for nobody could take her place. She seems contented now, and fortunately she has the six children to occupy her thoughts. Though pale, she is not wasted, and there is good reason to believe that this bow that did not break with the strain will [not] break with the recoil — The funeral was yesterday: not a happy one, but not such a funeral as the last or the last but one. Jane's funeral is not to be thought of. She was put in a charnel & not in the ground. We could never get near her. Now that horrible vault has been removed, and she lies *somewhere* under the grass, but there is no mark of the place. This was Charles's unhappy way. But it is better now than before. I could get nearer to her now and she is by herself. There ought to be no such grass as that which grows over Jane, and we ought to be able to see where she lies. It is against nature, a perverse philosophy that is simply wilful, to hide such a creature as Jane in the ground, without any sign, and I must feel wronged by it. —

I liked particularly to hear that you had said that you felt like a boy. You were always so young, though something better than a green boy! Let it be a boy of 22, which I remember was [?] a fine age, and lasted a long time. I have had my fears that you would come back older, and since you help to keep me young, — *younger*, I should age fast. I like to hear of the next presidential campaign, though I fear and expect that the Republicans will take steps back rather than forward, and that we shall have to hear of North & South instead of civil service. I like to hear of the campaign that's coming, because the song *I* shall sing will be — Saw ye Jamie coming? quo' he — Saw ye Jamie comin (with the grandees by his side, and a' the drums & drummin!)

I mean now to go to work. I have no lectures before me and nothing else that ought to thwart me. I do want about 6000 dollars to finish my collection — which you will like when you see it — but it is a very comfortable[?] one now, and very conveniently arranged for me, by Winsor's directions. Can't you make somebody collect the ballads in other parts of Spain as they have been collected in Catalonia (and Portugal)? A word from an ambassador to a man like Gayangos (is he in Madrid?) and passed by G. to some enterprising young fellows in one province and another, might have a good effect. The popular ballads that are collected *now* are of the universal sort, you know, and considerably more to my purpose than the romancero ballads. As lyrics, I don't think there is anything better anywhere than some of the Catalan. There must be a great lot that could be recovered in Spain — no country more likely to be rich in them. And they are well preserved, with beautiful burdens, and all the popular charm — so different from Italy, where mostly the ballads have lost their wild grace. — Well, dear Jamie, I wish I could be sure that you two were happy together today, and I have no objection to throwing in your secretary, since I hear he has been a good fellow. None the less do I wish I had been your secretary for the nonce. Love to Mrs. Lowell and perfect health soon. We think of you constantly and I never see Grace, and I see her often, without a talk about you.

Your loving F. C. ever.

Cambridge, Nov. 9, [1879]
Sunday

Dearest Jamie,

I hear all that you write to Grace N., and we never meet without talking all the late news over. Though there must be intervals of a week or two, and more I suppose, between your letters from America, there are no long intervals in our thoughts about you. We feel how much it means, when you say what would I give to see Cambridge Common! Though it is impossible for me, who was born in Boston & lived there 17 years, to feel native to Cambridge as you do, yet all but my earliest heartstrings are twined round this place. And then the lonesomeness of Madrid! We all say, were it but Paris, London, or even Dresden! But I must fill this bit of paper with something that will change your thoughts for five minutes, if I can. First then, you would be glad to see Grace. She has come out of that long strain upon her health and her heart, unimpaired as to one and stronger in the other. I should lack voice should I try to speak Grace's true praises. She has been herself, her mother's daughter, Jane's sister (feminine for Sidney's sister) and herself besides. There has been no end to her patience, sweetness, tenderness, devotion, no beginning to repining, fainting, selfconsidering, and now she is quite cheerful. Her great care now seems to be you. There are depths in Grace that never will be fathomed. I thought I knew her (she maintains fiercely that nobody knows anybody else, that the fondest heart & next our own is not sensibly nearer to understanding us than the stranger) but though all I have learned of her before stands for authentic & undisproved, I discover wide regions that I knew nothing of. — Charles was here yesterday on a matter of probate, and he told me that he and Grace would have about 3000 a year each, besides the house and furniture (which go to the one that lives longer) and their shares of the land. C. is fairly well but tires himself at times and has to stop. It is a pain in the back of his head that he feels, and this comes from lecturing two successive hours ex tempore. —

Cambridge seems particularly still. The professors don't make much stir in the learned world. Goodwin has a Greek grammar coming out in England & is helping with a Greek lexicon, & Lane has almost finished a Latin grammar: but how little we do, now that we have lost you. Perhaps I ought to count, and be proud to count, the labors of the young chemists

42

on ortho-brombenzyl compounds (think of this replacing ortho-doxy!) and "the relative replacebility (sic) of the bromine in the three brombenzyl-bromides." Alas! three brombenzyl-bromides in the place[?] of the three old faculties! Does not that to a narrow minded man look like tapering to a very fine point? — I am among the guilty ones that do nothing though I animadvert on the president for making halls and donations his themes instead of achievements in letters and science at commencement. — A day or two I thought we were in great luck. A Mr Walter Hastings was said to have left H. C. properties that in the end would amount to 800,000 dollars. The sum has gone down to half a million, and nearly half of that is to be spent on a *hall* — (from 200000 to 250000) that we don't want — and in the college yard, where we have no room for more. — Sever Hall is built & looks comely, but I fancy the rooms will be dark. — We have just had an election, preceeded [sic] by the usual caucuses. We could not do better than nominate Wentworth Higginson. I for one had much to swallow. He will be sure to agitate for woman's suffrage. He, Phillips, Julia Howe, Lucy Stone & Mrs. Stanton have been replying to Frank Parkman in the N. A. Review on that matter, and a glance at their papers seemed to me to show that at least five of them were necessary to make even a faint fight.[31] I saw John Holmes at a caucus. He expects you as sure as a Cornish man does Arthur. May we all live to meet!

Dinner rings. I mean to drop you a line often. Love to Mrs. Lowell. Were this world in my power I would come & stay the winter with you.

Always your faithful & loving
Ciarli.

Hon. James R. Lowell, Madrid.

The Fields referred to at the beginning of the next letter are Mr and Mrs John W. Field, American friends of Lowell, who lived much in Europe. Field himself has already been mentioned as a correspondent of Grace Norton.

We learn from Lowell's letter of December 30 that the specimen ballad sent by Child 'care of Uncle Sam' was 'Gil Brenton,' published in Part I of *The English and Scottish Popular Ballads*, December 1882.

Cambridge, 21 Dec 1879.
Dearest Jamie,

Now that the Fields are with you one gets the outside view which no Spaniard and no transient American could give. We are assured that your

[31] See the *North American Review*, November 1879, for 'The Other Side of the Woman Question,' in dissent from Francis Parkman's article, 'The Woman Question,' in the October issue.

spirits are not broken, for which gratias agimus. Of comfort for your poor wife indeed we hear not much — all the mending is to be so slow and the recovery so far off. You have new Cuban troubles on your hands now, and I fear your diplomacy will require a good deal of attention. When did you look into a book? I mean a book that *is* a book — such as a metrical romance, cants de la tera, & that ilk? Shall I comfort you by telling you what you escape here? You escape seeing preparations for re-nominating Grant, among which preparations, we may say, is all sorts of dodging to avoid prosperity by stopping legal-tender. But you read your Nation. I mention this only because it makes me fierce as ten furies. After all, is it better to be under Dizzy and have Afghan wars on one's mind?

I sent you the other day an Advertiser with an account of Dr Holmes' 70 birthday. Let not the consequence be to make you stay away till after that date is passed for you. To be set up at a breakfast table with all the past and present Atlantic fry in front of you and around you, each ready to pronounce a decided compliment — would it not make a man's hair turn white in a single night? John said the best things, I thought. There were many new names not belonging to this eastern clime, and so the occasion was not so characteristic of St Botolphston as some old symposiums: it was not a symposium at all, but a *composium*. Nevertheless in far off Madrid, cold perhaps, shady probably, foreign altogether, even an Advertiser must have a faintly agreeable taste — The advertisements are there: some of these are very new too, but you could find India Wharf & Long Wharf, and *horse-sales* — don't you love those? the horse not afraid of anything — but afraid of spile-drivers? Raciness in the Advertiser remains no where else but in the horse columns. Have you noticed how the fellows that write fire-works advertisements are going out, perhaps gone out? Had Boston known what was for its peace, it would always keep up that 4th of July show for the genius that the institution fostered. It was fully equal to Sir Thos. Malory. Now a race has come that know not Jacob — Boston is not Boston. New England is not half N. E. with you out of it. — I sent you too, care of Uncle Sam, a ballad set up, the first that came to hand almost, but a sort of average as to length. I have been talking with Houghton & Osgood about printing, and they have written to Macmillan. If it were not for the trouble I would rather deal only with some English publisher, for I want, if I can, to make a ballad-book that will last, and something depends on its having the right godfather. I work now every day on this matter, and sometimes am in good spirits about it sometimes very low.

A recent discovery of an Odinic song in Shetland has excited me very much. I have written the person[?] said to be the right man, to ask what hope there is of ballads. It seems to me that they must linger there. They spread like Norway rats, and there is plenty of Norway in the Orkneys & Shetland. Very likely my man will say there is nothing — just as a world renowned cryptogamic botanist in Sweden had never seen lichens which

44

Tuckerman picked up as he was approaching the man's house. — I almost said I would come out: but I reflected upon the state of my pocket, and asked — had I not better spend the £50 it would cost me for the sea passages in buying the help of some poor Shetland schoolmasters or parsons? Only if I were on the spot — that is on the 20 or 30 inhabited islands — I could be continually prodding up the people. There *must* be ballads there: — how else have the people held out against poverty, cold & darkness? Kristensen, a Danish schoolmaster, in three years, about 1870, gathered in a very small district in Jutland 150 ballads, one half of which had never been known to be in tradition, & 14 were utterly unknown. Do I talk like a feller trying to get stock taken in copper-mines? The Calumet & Hecla is 275 — why should the "Security" be 5? Hasn't the Lord done as well by one man as by another? Surely there is a vein for the silver & a place for gold where they *find* it. Iron is taken out of the earth & brass is molten out of the stone. We will see what Laurenson says — Laurenson of Lerwick, Leog House, Lerwick — beyond John o' Groats, beyond the Orkneys. Were you careless and I richer, I would try to make you meet me there. The summer is pleasant — there is 3 months of afternoon — the people primitive. How I wish we could do it! —

Grace Norton goes out a little — went to Boston to dine on Friday. She does all she can to make the world seem like a world, but it never will again. There is no news here unless I tell you that Lane's pretty little daughter, Louisa, is engaged to one of the Albany van Rensellaers. — While I think of it, why don't you let *Romania* come to you from Paris this year? It is always well worth seeing. I can make the college take it by mail instead of annually. I have all your numbers safe. Two were lost in the mail, but I have supplied the gaps. — The Printing Clubs would be glad to have you pay your subscriptions since 1877. They have suffered from the bad times. I thought it not worth the while to have the books accumulating while you were gone, but the Secy now asks me to get such arrears as I can. If you care enough about the matter, you could send to the enclosed addresses the sums mentioned, with directions to have books sent to my care. It would be a help to the societies. — What will you do for Christmas? I have been reading your Sir L.[aunfal] with a class of girls in *my* girls school. Though you never were the scornful young knight, you seemed to me, seen through the winter, almost as lonely as the knight returned from the quest. Happier Christmas — love to your wife — kindest remembrances to Mr & Mrs. Field.

Thy loving Ciarli

Mem.
Chaucer Socy *1878. 9. 80*
     45 shils each year, including postage
Early Eng. Text. *both* series, 45   "
New Shakspere 24   "

You would be in for   6 x 45   270
                         3 x 24   72
£ 17/2, a big sum!   342

New Shakspere £ 3/12 to Arthur G. Snelgrove, Esq.
London Hospital, E.
W. A. Dalziel, the rest. [address label for Dalziel attached]

Legacion de los Estados Unidos
   de America en España
   ——————
                                           30 December, 1879.
     Particular

Dear Ciarli,

how deeply grateful I feel for the love & sympathy of your letters I need not say. I had not the heart to answer them out of the darkness in which I was sitting when they came; but they brought you so near that they were a very tender consolation. Now the time seems to have come when I can say with some feeling of security that Fanny is better, though I am grown so timidly superstitious that I hardly dare to write it. Twice, after beginning to hope, there have been frightful relapses, & I understand perfectly the feeling which made the Greeks try to appease certain mysterious powers by calling them Wellmeaning, as our ancestors called them Good Folk. For more than a fortnight now that infinitely dear woman has been herself — you will know how much that means — the old light of love has come back into her eyes & she has been gaining steadily (if very slowly) in strength & hope. It will be a long while yet before she will be able to leave her bed or even to change her position in it, but at least there is manifest improvement. I cannot write what we have gone through, some day when we get back to paradise I will tell you. Twice it has seemed as if she could not hold out through the night & twice she has been brought to me like Alcestis from the grave. Nothing but such a constitution as she had inherited from a pure New England ancestry could have carried her through. There were long weeks when she was wholly alienated from all she loved, but now she takes a touching interest in all that was dear to her before, & we talk over the grandchildren again. To me she is inexpressibly tender, & it is as if we had been just betrothed anew. The old nobleness of her nature reveals itself at every turn. I cannot thank God enough.

I will try when I can pull myself together again to see if I can get you any inedited folksongs. But I greatly doubt. The Spaniards are singularly indifferent to such things if not contemptuous of them. There is almost no scholarship here in our sense of the word & most of the criticism is in the good old *isimo* style. So entire & stupid a selfsatisfaction I never saw in any people. Why, they positively brag of Trafalgar. The *penitus divisos ab orbe Britannos* were nothing to them in point of seclusion from the rest of mankind. But I love the jades for a' that — perhaps on account of a' that. I shout with laughter over their newspapers sometimes. For example the *Imparcial* (a very clever paper by the way) had an article not long [ago] on "Longevity in Europe" based on one by Max Waldstein in a Viennese Review. Here is a bit of it. "Salimos los españoles los menos aventajados en eso de vivir mucho tiempo; pero *como es necesario dudar siempre de la veracidad de los extranjeros en todo cuanto atañe á nuestro pais* &c &c Isn't that delicious? Commonly they bluntly attribute this malice of facts to envy. They fancy themselves always in the age of Charles V, & the perfect gravity with which they always assume the airs of a Great Power is not without a kind of pathetic dignity. We all wink at the little shifts of a decayed gentleman, especially when he is Don Quixote as this one certainly is. They are full of humour, by the way, & their stories are wonderfully good. Some day I will tell you their version of *Am I Giles or am I not?* which is much better than ours. The naïve profanity with which they treat sacred subjects — even the Crucifixion — in their newspapers I attribute to there being a large majority among their *literators*[?] of descendants from *conversos*. One observation I have made but cannot explain — their insensibility to noise. They seem even to be fond of it. It implies, I suppose, either a low civilization or peculiarly healthy nerves.

I have just been in to see Fanny (for I go to bed now that we have an English nurse) & she looks nicely. I cannot bear to tell you all she has had to suffer — among other things her right arm painfully helpless & the hand swollen with what seems to be rheumatic gout — & she bears it all with heroic cheerfulness. O altitudo! The beautiful clear depths there are in such a woman's nature!

I have a *tolerable* Catalan Dictionary now — too large for the post — but I shall bring it home. How I long to have that dear familiar earth under my feet! And somehow I think it longs for me too. Good bye, beloved. Give my love to Grace & tell her I shall write soon. I have less loose time than you would think Thanks for *Gil Brenton* which I knew must be your's or the Devil's. I was delighted to think you were going on with the work which nobody can do so well.

Give my love to Mrs Child & the children who I suppose are grown out of all cry by this time.

Your affectionate

J. R. L

Child's birthday letter of 1880 salutes the new Minister to the Court of St James's. Lowell's appointment to the highest post in the United States diplomatic service had come, unsought, in January. The ensuing five years in England were the high point of his public career.

Lowell was actually still in Madrid when Child wrote, but made a preliminary visit to England in March, leaving Mrs Lowell in the care of the Fields. Though she had a serious relapse during his absence, he was able to escort her to London the following month.

The sonnet mentioned by Child was included in *Heartsease and Rue* (1888), the last volume of Lowell's verse to appear within his lifetime, but the other set of verses has not been traced.

Feb. 22, 1880.

My dear Jamie,

Though my head is spinning with some hepatic disturbance, I am not going to let the 22d pass without making my bow at the legation. But under which king, Bezonian? Are you in London or in Madrid? The newspapers, that knew all your privacy a month ago, tell us nothing now. We know that the nobility & gentry were arranging receptions for you throughout England — that you had taken a place in the Isle of Wight — & had had an audience appointed at Osborne — but we do not know where you are. So it is to be Hyde Park & not Cambridge Common — Rotten Row & not Harvard Row — and the earliest sight we shall have of you will be a year and a half from now. Yet you cannot like it — I tell everybody you do not — and when you come back you will say, multum fuit incola anima mea. But I will whine no more. — Your last letter was written in the heyday of youth, and today you will scarce be more than one and twenty. If I thought you felt older than in 79, I could not write to you so cheerfully. But your life is rejuvenated even by your coming out of the shadow which lay along your path for six long months. To have you write as you did seemed almost to atone for your long suffering: and no doubt the last half year in Madrid may be sweet to remember by and by. But how terrible was the reality! Even here, 4000 miles and fourteen days off, the oppression to our spirits was dreadful — our ignorance, our inability to come to you, to help you any way: and when I say you, I mean both of you. —

Well, we have not much to say of ourselves. In comparison with your experiences, ours have been of no account. Charles N. has had a great deal of trouble with his head from overworking. He gives two lectures extempore thrice a week, and the strain is great. Then come a host of examination books. He bears all with his habitual patience & pluck. — The best sign in you was your beginning to relish versing. I thought the sonnet to the young English girl playing on the cittern very charming, and wished you had made your secretary write out the verses on the stolen turkey[?]. —

I suppose you have not kept any sort of a journal in Spain: I wish you would in England — even if you jot down mere anecdotes. The other day, happening to take up Gillies' Memoirs, I found in the first pages your favorite bourd of "nae wale o wigs". There was another story of the same laird which I wanted to share with you. Perhaps you know it. He had been

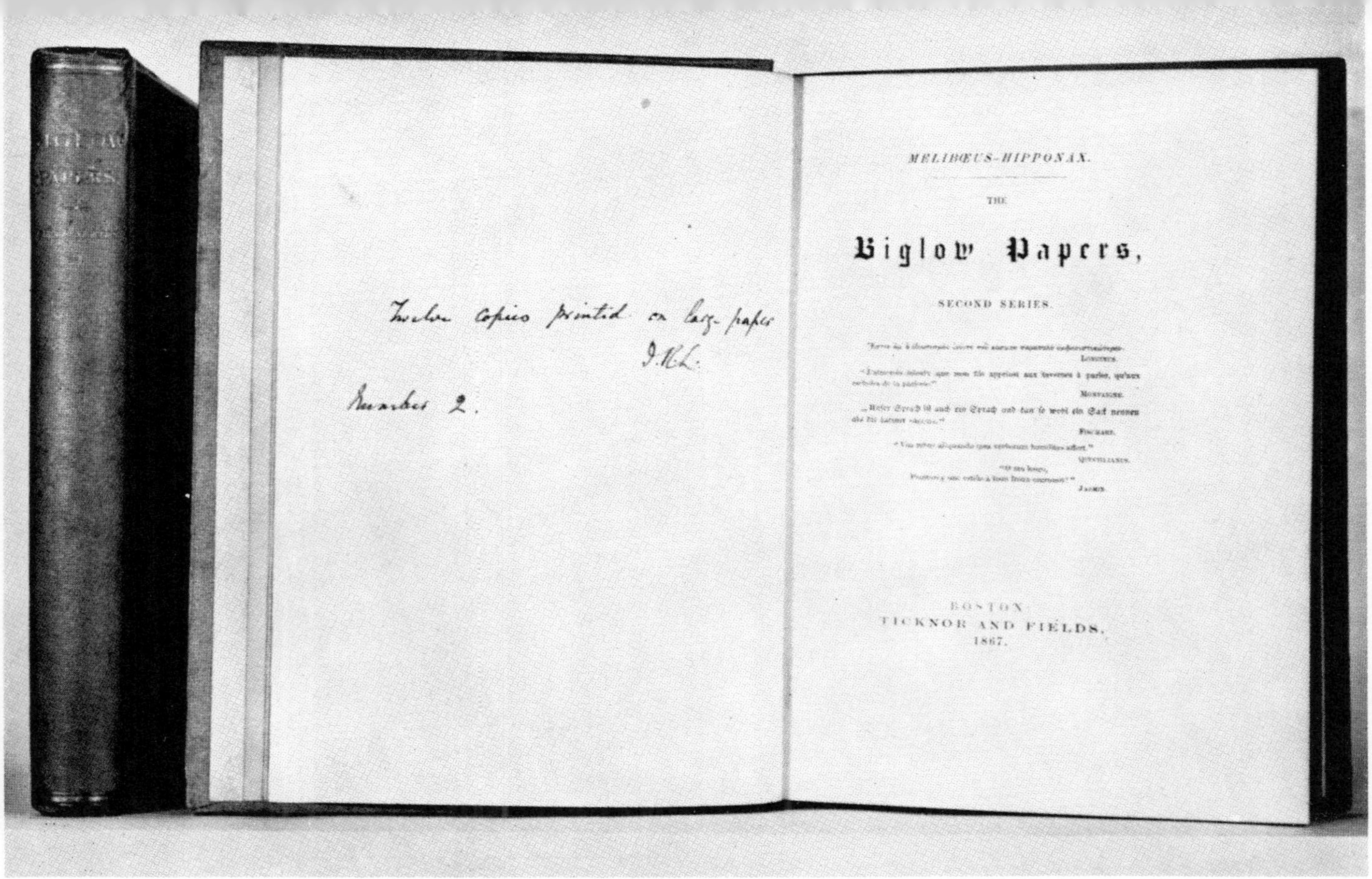

PLATE V

THE LARGE-PAPER COPIES OF *The Biglow Papers* GIVEN CHILD BY LOWELL

PLATE VI

CHILD CARICATURED BY WILLIAM JAMES

PLATE VIIb

LOWELL IN LATER LIFE

PLATE VIIa

CHILD IN LATER LIFE

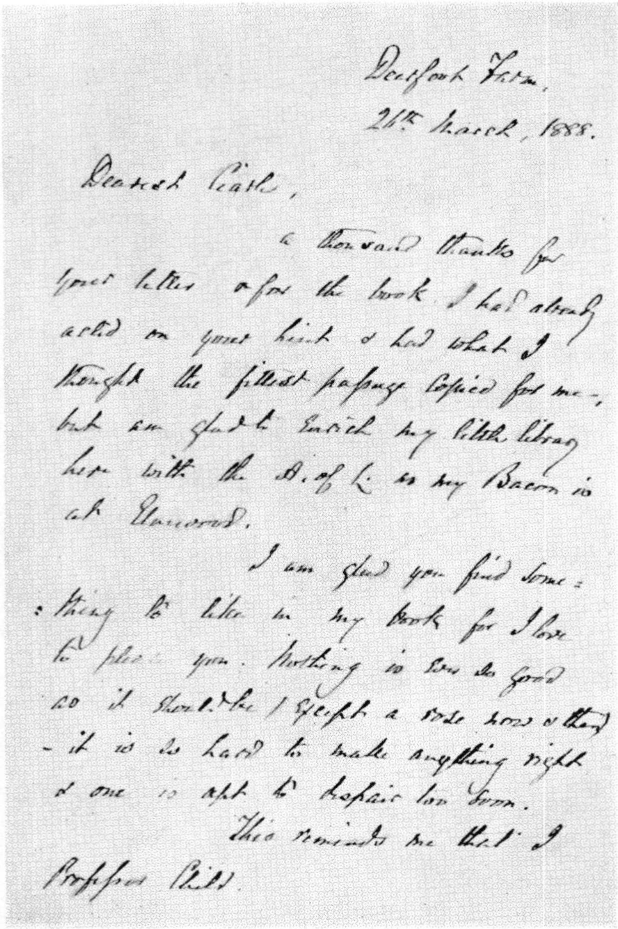

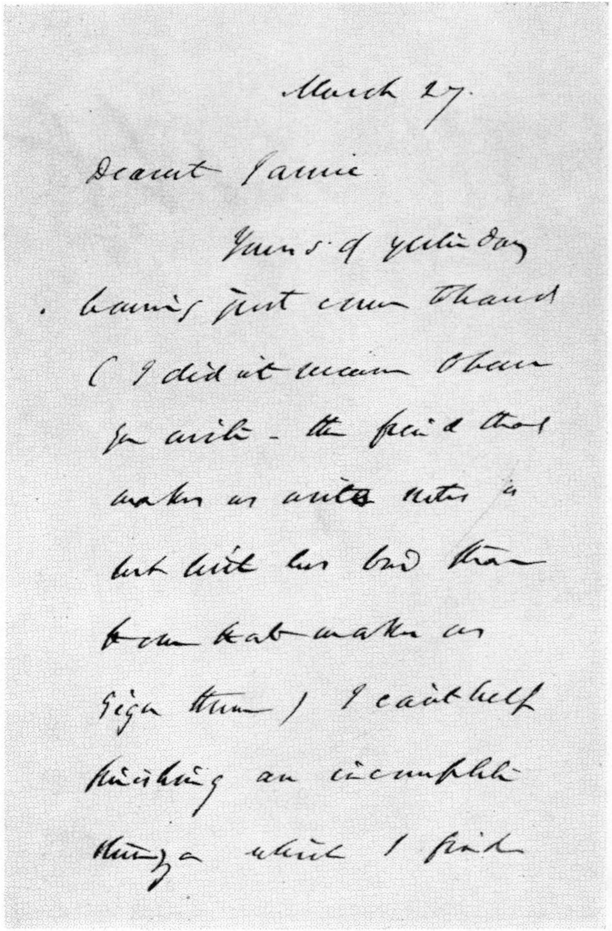

having a heavy rouse, and the servant, when he came in the next morning, told him it was an awfu' morning, & he had better not get up. "Is it an *awfu'* morning." "Ay, that it is." "Weel, make up the fire in the parlor, steck the shutters, put the punch bowl on the table, etc. etc. and we'll see *what kind o' nicht it will make.* —

Adieu, dear man. I'm verra glad, since you are to stay, that it is to be in England. Indeed I ought to care for nothing now that you are once more in hope. May there be a straight course to health. Love to the ambassadress. I wish I could have something chanted for her in a cathedral — se fossi io amico del Re dell' universo! [32] — ohimè!

Ever your loving

F. Ciarli.

When the correspondence is resumed, after an interval of more than a year, Lowell answers a letter of Child's which apparently has disappeared. As Minister, Lowell was of course in a strategic position to further Child's unwearied pursuit of ballads, and we have here some of the early moves in a transatlantic game that is played with zest on both sides for the next three and a half years. The second Earl Granville, once again Minister for Foreign Affairs, and John Francis Campbell of Islay, author of *Popular Tales of the West Highlands*, prove themselves valuable intermediaries.

The 'gloomy telegrams' are concerned with President Garfield's precarious state; shot by Guiteau on July 2, he lingered on until September 19.

Legation of the United States

London

17th August, 1881.

Dear Ciarli,

Your letter, as you can well conceive, brought me pain & pleasure. I was glad to see your handwriting again & to hear that you were well & had not forgotten me as I deserved or seemed to deserve. I have owed you a letter I know not how long, but it is harder than ever to write here. So many people write to me that during the season I have sometimes had twenty five notes to answer before I went out of a morning & half as many more when I came

---

[32] Cf. Paolo and Francesca to Dante, *Inferno*, V, 91–93:

Se fosse amico il re de l' universo,
Noi pregheremmo lui de la tua pace,
Poi c' hai pietà del nostro mal perverso.

home in the afternoon. Even were I not dining out, I cannot write in the evening on account of my eyes, which are as old — as I am. Never mind, I am writing to you now & loving you as always. . . .

I wrote to Lord Granville this morning (he is Campbell of Islay's brother-in-law) asking him to use his *benevolence* in the matter of your letter & to give my pledge for you. I do not remember to have met Mr Campbell. He has sold Islay to a distiller, by the way.

We are in the midst & at the mercy of gloomy telegrams again. I still cling to hope — encouraged by my dreadful experience in Madrid. Once we had a wholly innumerable pulse. I hate to remember it. Write again when you feel like it & be sure that you are always the dear Ciarli of so many years. Fanny has gone to North Wales. She cannot yet walk as well as could be wished, but otherwise is well & happy. I suppose a new Administration would mean my recall, but I should stay here till next summer at any rate.

Your affectionate old friend
J. R. L.

In the birthday letter for 1882 begins the patient stalking of the Scottish baronet who turns out to be Sir Hugh Hume Campbell, and whose 'two manuscript vols. of ballads' ultimately make a significant contribution to Child's *magnum opus* — the publication of which is now finally contracted for.

The 'mortal season' had carried away Mrs Henry James, mother of William and Henry, William Henry Bellows, the minister, and Richard Henry Dana the younger, who, ironically, had failed of Senate confirmation for the post now occupied by Lowell when appointed by Grant six years before.

James G. Blaine had resigned as Secretary of State following President Garfield's death, but had continued to serve, at the request of the new President, Arthur, until December. During the remainder of Lowell's ministership his chief was Frederick T. Frelinghuysen.

Feb. 22, 1882.

Dearest Jamie,

I wonder whether they leave you your birth-day to yourself. Owing to snow-bondage, I have seen none of those who are wont to celebrate the 22d on this side: but I have little doubt that Charles, though he is all but knocked up with the epidemic cold, has written you a word. Were professors what they should be, we should have had all the cables to ourselves and might have sent you living messages instead of dead letters. — Here's a bumper — dulci digne mero! — and may you be feeling as immortal as you always have looked, when you have *not* had twinges in your chest — and of those we have heard nothing for years.

I must tell you that you did me a real service by speaking to Lord Granville: for his brother in law, Campbell of Islay, immediately began to be interested in my affairs. He wrote me from Mull, from Edinburgh, London, from everywhere, and both sent me a few things which he had and tried to get something from other folk. I have let him alone for the winter — he always go [sic] to some end of the world, Scandaroon, Boothia Felix, or Mountains of the Moon: but when he returns to Niddry Lodge, then I must beat him up: for his last word was that he had found a Scottish gentleman who possessed a fine old house & *two manuscript vols. of ballads*! This Scot would not let me know his name — did not wish to be persecuted by "collectors": but would have a judge look over his MSS., and if they would suit me, *perhaps* let me have what I wanted. I am very sorry he did not give the name, for I should have asked my country's representative, in case of his coming in contact with this baronet, and finding a molle tempus, to recommend me to his grace, and have no doubt that my ambassador would prevail. — After many postponements, I came to terms with Houghton three or four months ago, and they should even now be setting up the everlasting old truck: but first it was type & then it was paper, and they have not begun. —

Do you know, my dear boy, what a mortal season this has been? Four names of good *old* Boston, were in the column of Deaths in one morning of last week! And here we have lost Mrs. James, who was to me & mine beyond all price and is beyond all replacing. In New York Bellows — the old minister of my wife's family, and in Rome, Dana. — Had you been here you would have been beset to go to Chicago to the Harvard Club dinner. Eliot went and took three men with him. Straight upon that followed invitations to New York & Philadelphia. You don't have to go *quite* a thousand miles, but then you do go to a thousand dinners. And my heart fails if I am asked to one. I faint too before half a dozen letters — and you cope calmly with two dozen a day. . . .

Your President, Arthur, has done unexpectedly well so far, and really seems to have assumed dignity and conscience with his high office. I suppose Blaine leaves you lots of sequelae of trouble. Here politics are very quiet. The President's death hushed all the more boisterous passions, and still operates perhaps.

Understand, my dear friend, that I *expect* no letters from you. I hope to live to see you come back. I wish I could come to Europe and see you in Switzerland on a vacation. But I don't look to any such pleasure. — I am sure that if you see Campbell you will *prod* him a bit, to keep up his benevolence in my behalf. The next time I speak to you of Ballads, I ought to have a good bit printed. — Give faithful love & remembrance to Mrs. Lowell, and continue your kindness ever to your affectionate

                                                            Ciarli.

The first of the ultimately ten parts of *The English and Scottish Popular Ballads* was published late in December 1882, with a dedication to Frederick J. Furnivall which was a graceful rejoinder to the dedication to Child of the Hales and Furnivall edition of the Percy folio fifteen years earlier. Lowell's presentation copy, with an inscription that he found too formal, reached him promptly, as the following letter shows.

Photographs of the scholar friends as they appeared in these later years are shown in Plate VII, reproduced from originals in the Harvard Archives. Lowell's description of himself is well substantiated.

The 'revulsion in our politics' was the revulsion against the abuses of the long Republican domination that was to culminate in the election of Cleveland in 1884. Early marks of the revulsion were the Democratic landslide in the off year of 1882 and the subsequent passage by a chastened Congress in 'lame duck' session of the Pendleton Act for the regulation of civil service. Implicit in Lowell's writing here is a position which received its definitive expression in his Reform Club address of 1888, 'The Place of the Independent in Politics.'

10, Lowndes Square.
S. W.

2nd Feb: 1883.

Dear Ciarli,

thank you over & over again for your beautiful book, the only fault I can find with which is the "Esq" you have added to my name & which seems to hold me at arm's length from you, as it were. But I won't be held there, do what you will!

I have been reading it with delight & wonder. The former you will understand better than anybody; the latter, called forth by the enormous labour you have spent on it you will be modestly incredulous about. You have really built an imperishable monument & I rejoice as heartily as the love I bear you gives me the right in having lived to see its completion. I did not know you were to begin printing so soon & I wish my name to appear on the list of subscribers as it ought. I hope it is not too late. I am particularly gratified with the dedication which will delight Furnivall & which he in all ways so truly deserved.

I am getting old & my beard has now more white than brown in it, but I on the whole enjoy my life here & feel that in some ways I have been & am useful. London I like beyond measure. The wonderful movement of life here acts as a constant stimulus — & I am beginning to need one. The climate also suits me better than any I ever lived in. I have only to walk a

52

hundred yards from my door to see green grass & hear the thrushes sing all winter long. These are a constant delight & I sometimes shudder to think of the poor dead weeds & grasses I have seen shivering in the castiron earth at home. But I shall come back to them to comfort them out of my own store of warmth with as hearty a sympathy as ever.

I need not tell you how glad I was of the revulsion in our politics. I think we shall keep all the ground we have won & before long bring the country forward or back to better ways. If not, I see no hope. Spain shows us to what a civil service precisely like our own will bring a country that ought to be powerful & prosperous. It wasn't the Inquisition, nor the expulsion of Jews or Moriscoes, but simply the Boss System that has landed Spain where she is.

Give my love to all who care for it & be sure that I am always as I have always been

Most affectionately yours
J. R. L.

Feb. 22, 1883.

My dear Jamie,

I have no thought of keeping at arm's length from you, not even a suspicion that you wished such a thing, and if I said Esq it was for those that might stand by. I was much refreshed by your note of twenty days ago. Any praise which you think it right to give me, on any score, is enjoyed as much as it is valued. I feared and fear that the book must be accounted very dull, for my spirits have been much worse than that for a long time. The mass of matter was very oppressive when I thought how little time might be left me, and if I had not been afraid to wait, I would have pushed into the Slavic territory and have forestalled some just criticism. But now I am going on to finish the other seven parts as well as I can in the shortest practicable time. I must not be careless, but must still less be fussy. Many is the time when I should like to have you by to answer me a question.

Your note to Lord Granville on my behalf was of great service. Campbell of Islay immediately began to show a considerable interest in my objects. I think he is a good fellow. He wrote me, it is now all but a year, that he knew a Scotch baronet who had a fine house and two manuscript volumes of ballads, and this Scotchman had said that he would have his ballads looked at, & if they suited my purpose would *perhaps* let me have them. But not a hair have we advanced since then. The baronet would not have his name known, for fear of "collectors"! I tell you this just because it may accidentally transpire who the man is. If I knew his name, I would have him addressed through others whom he might heed.

Campbell of Islay sent me a very good modern ballad, almost as well done as Old Robin Gray, very unaffectedly simple, beginning

53

O Randal was a bonnie lad
When he gaed awa,
A bonnie, bonnie lad was he
When he gaed awa.

He learned it from the singing of Lady Archibald Campbell. You may hear of it some day when you are visiting. I want to secure the *notes* extremely, and if I ever do shall send them & the words to our friend Mrs. Webb of Portland. Keep an ear open, and should there be a molle tempus fandi perhaps some charming Mollie[?] will write the notes off for you — for what wad they not do for you, Jamie!

You will like the ballad very much.

We have had a hard winter. C. N. has had much to bear, I some rheumatism. Your thrushes I am hearkening for. The hardy sparrows have not felt the penalty of Adam. Now the sun has a springy motion in his gait, & we can see till almost six in the afternoon, & while I listen for a bird I speir for a snow drop. But when you think of the contrast of the Februaries, how can you think of coming back to ours!

But this 22d is a little conscious of what it ought to be. There is no summer bird singing in the haunch of winter, but the clouds take on gay tints and the world has a look of hope. I expect to keep two or three more before I see you. Perhaps I shall have all my seven *Parts* out of the way and have nothing to do but bring up these years with you.

Why do you think of becoming a subscriber? You cant find room for two copies of so big a book in your house. Be content. Thou owest me no subscription, I never gave thee kingdoms, nor even a poor volume.

What you say of white in your beard is hardest of all to imagine. It must be fashion, there is no other way of accounting for it. I see by your writing that you are still of no age, of Adam's years. Give my faithful remembrances to Mrs. Lowell, and continue to be my good lord, as I am thy loving servant ever,

Ciarli

In June 1883, as will be seen, the campaign for the Campbell ballads was brought to a triumphant conclusion, in a great convergence of 'influences' involving Lord Granville, the eleventh Baron Reay, Campbell of Islay, and Charles Eliot Norton, who was in England for the summer.

Adee, the parcel-literary man, is Alvey Augustus Adee, Assistant Secretary of State from 1882 until his death in 1924. It was he who turned over the Madrid legation to Lowell in 1877 and who wrote an introduction for a selection from Lowell's Spanish dispatches published in 1899.

Legation of the United States
London

11th June, 1883.

Dear Child,

a day or two ago I got a note from Lord Granville to say that you could have the Hugh Campbell collection of Ballads. This morning Lord Reay brought them to my house, & it appears that Charles Norton had written to him about it & that being a neighbour of Sir Hugh's *he* had asked for & got them. So I know not what share Campbell of Isla had in the matter, but I believe you are in correspondence with him & can thank him as if nothing had happened in the way of other intervention. I have asked Lord G. to thank him in the meanwhile. Whoever got 'em, I am heartily glad for your sake, dear old fellow.

I send them by our bag tomorrow to Washington as the safest method & as avoiding all question of Custom Houses. I shall write to Adee who is in the State Department & is a parcel-literary man, asking him to forward it to you & warn you of its coming. This is the only advantage I have yet reaped from being in the Diplomatic Service of my Country.

Fanny is better than she has ever been since our arrival in England. She doesn't go out except when she is obliged to be present in gilded palaces at the ceremonies of the crowned ghoules who devour this unhappy people. I am as well as a minister can be at the height of the season when the milk-&-waters are going over him which is a worse lot than the prophet's. But there is much that I really enjoy & much that amuses me.

I am become a sort of public institution here & hardly a week passes that I am not asked to preside at a meeting, to distribute prizes & the like. These are the hardships of my lot. I will not say what kind of public institution I liken myself to, lest you should think of Swift.

Most affectionately

Yours always

J. R. L.

Cambridge,
Aug. 8[?],
1883.

Care caput!

/ tantum minister quantum ministellus /

Those two volumes slipped into my hands at last — after eighteen months of waiting — with no more trouble than a falling blossom. I almost felt that I was the American nation personified. Adee was most kind, & wished even that I would send the books back by him, which strikes me however as no kindness to you. Campbell of Isla had the MSS in his hands for some days,

55

but would not wait for me to send him word what to do with them. I had written to him meanwhile, & to Sir Hugh Hume Campbell.

The ballads are not what they would have been two hundred years ago, but could not possibly be dispensed with now that I have undertaken to make a breade[?] of every rag the wild Muse ever wore. —

The good things you write of Mrs Lowell are cordial to my heart, which has been sorely depressed by loss of friends and calamities to friends.

I have been pumping Harry James, when I have met him, for the means of forming a conception how you live over there. He has helped me a little. I see something of your public existence in the reprints of the Advertiser, but not so much as I should like. Just now, being tired excessively, I fancy how fine it would be, when the season is over in London, to be with you for a month on some mountain top to which courtiers & couriers would not climb.

Charles Norton will bring some tidings of you soon. With love to Mrs Lowell, and begging you to keep many years for America, Ever yours,

faithfully & affectionately,

F. J. C.

J. R. Lowell Esq.   Legation of the U. S. A.
at London.

The search for a copy of *Les visions d'Oger*, set off by Paul Meyer of *Romania*, and figuring conspicuously in several ensuing letters, finally concluded successfully in one sense, in that the copy reported by Brunet to be in the Bibliothèque Nationale turned out to be there after all, in spite of Léopold Delisle and the Duc d'Aumale. Yet, on examination, the *Visions* contained nothing to clarify the relations between Thomas Rhymer and Ogier. This we learn from a supplementary note in the last part of the *Ballads*, published posthumously. In Part II, published in the summer of 1884, and containing 'Thomas Rhymer,' Child had been forced to report that none of his inquiries, 'though most courteously aided in France,' had resulted in the finding of a copy.[33]

On 22 November 1883 Lowell had been elected by the students Rector of the University of St Andrews, for the usual three-year term. Duties consisted largely of attending an installation and delivering an inaugural address. However, as the subsequent letter of Lowell sug-

[33] *The English and Scottish Popular Ballads* (Boston, 1882–98), I, 319, n.; V, 290. It was Professor W. H. Schofield who finally furnished Child with an abstract of the *Visions*.

gests, the legality of the election was challenged by the supporters of the defeated candidate, and the victor thereon withdrew, regretting, so he said, that 'Univ. Sanct. Andr. Scot. Dom. Rect.' would never appear after his name in the *Quinquennial Catalogue*. In his place the students elected Lord Reay, who had secured the Campbell ballads.[34]

At the time of Child's present letter Matthew Arnold had recently arrived for his first visit to the United States.

Cambridge   Nov 25[?] [1883]

Carissimum caput!

I did not mean that Ballads should give you any more trouble, lest you should think them worse than Paddy. This morning Paul Meyer sent me the enclosed, or one of the enclosed, and I could not very well help writing the other. If the Duc d'Aumale concedes the request, there will be no more bother for you than just to let me know. The chances I thought much greater if you seemed to vouch for me, by sending on my note with just one line saying that you know who I am.

The romance is that of Thomas of Erceldoun, from which comes our ballad of Thomas Rhymer. It will be very singular if Ogier turns out to be a prophet, and Thomas is one only at second hand. (The book is Les visions d'Oger au royaulme de Fairie (Le premier, second et troisième livre des visions d'Oger le Dannoys, etc. Paris, 1542)

I have begun printing Part II, and can hardly at best get a copy in time for anything but an appendix. It may also turn out that Ogier's visions are nought to Thomas. But I ought to look into the matter.

This morning I hear that you are to be rector of St Andrew's. It will not surprise us to see you primate, chancellor and "Lord High" of all England. Was there ever such a series of conquests, triumphs, sports, since Caesar? And legitimate too.

As Rector of St Andrews, thou art naturally lord of all Scotland. Let thy first decree be that every ballad known to any lady, maidservant, fishwife, dairywoman or nurse be given up under penalties of misprision & praemunire to all that shall be art & part in the withholding of the same. We have Matthew Arnold reading his poems all about. He has not many lectures & was melancholy about his voice, but they say he has drawn well. Hoping that I do not annoy thee overmuch

Ever thine faithfully
F. J. C.

James Russell Lowell, Esq.   London.

[34] Letter to James B. Thayer, 24 December 1883 (*Letters of James Russell Lowell*, III, 108); *Rectorial Addresses Delivered at the University of St. Andrews*, ed. William Knight (London, 1894), pp. xxiv–xxvi.

Child's pleasure in the Du Maurier version of 'The Golden Vanity' fully justified the trouble taken by the busy Minister in copying it off at the head of the following letter.[35] The version duly found its place among the variants of the ballad in the published work, 'as sung by Mr George Du Maurier, sent me by J. R. Lowell.'[36]

Lowell's perennial vigilance on behalf of the College Library was in the case of Fergusson's book unnecessary: the Library had purchased a copy of the second edition in 1876.

The great Cambridge scholar Henry Bradshaw, in some respects an English counterpart of Child himself, but whose career lacked a similar crown of tangible accomplishment, has already appeared in the correspondence, in connection with the Chaucerian discussions of 1870.

The conclusion of Lowell's note of December 20 suggests that he was feeling premonitions of the Cleveland victory then still nearly a year in the future.

10, Lowndes Square.
S. W.

[December 1883]

> There was a gallant ship, a gallant ship was she,
>   Hic diddledee for the Lowlands low,
> And she went by the name of the *Golden Vanitee*,
>   As she sailed for the Lowlands low.
>
> And she hadna sailed a league, a league or barely three,
>   When she fell in with the French Gallee.
>
> Then up spoke the cabinboy & up spoke he,
>   Hic &c
> "What'll ye gie me an I sink the French gallee?"
>   As she &c
>
> Then up spoke the Captain & up spoke he,
> "I'll gie ye an estate in the North Countree."
>
> "Then roll me up tight in a black bullskin,
> And throw me overboard, sink or swim!"
>
> They rolled him up tight in a black bull skin,
> And threw him overboard, sink or swim.

[35] Printed, without the ballad and with other omissions, in *Letters of James Russell Lowell*, III, 110–111, as from '31 Lowndes Square, 1884.'

[36] *English and Scottish Popular Ballads*, V, 135 ff. (in Pt. IX, published September 1894).

And awa' & awa' & awa' swam he
Till he swam up to the French Gallee.

And some were playing cards & some were playing dice
He just took out a gimlet & bored sixty holes & thrice.

And some they ran with cloaks & some they ran with caps
But they couldna run awa' from the saltwater drops.

Then awa' & awa' & awa' swam he
Till he swam back to the Gowden Vanitee.

"Now throw me o'er a rope & pull me up aboard,
And prove unto me as good as your word!"

"I'll na throw ye o'er a rope, I'll na pull ye up aboard,
I'll na prove unto thee as good as my word!"

"An ye na throw me o'er a rope, an ye na pull me up aboard,
I'll just sink ye as I sank the French Gallee!"

So they threw him o'er a rope & they pulled him up aboard,
    Hic &c
And they proved unto him as good as their word.
    As they sailed &c

Dear Ciarli,

    the foregoing is a ballad that du Maurier sings with grand pathos & expression. It occurred to me that it might be useful to you as an illustration in some odd corner, so I asked him for a copy & there it is. I could not bear to part with his ms. because he had illustrated it with a humourous drawing having a personal reference in it. I hope the ballad may be of some good to you & that you do not know it by heart already as you do all the rest.

    When I got up this morning it was snowing & I had been lying for some time watching the flakes fluttering up & down like the ghosts of moths seeking vainly the flowers they used to pillage, & thinking of home as I always do when it snows. Almost my earliest recollection is of a snowstorm & putting crumbs on the windowsill for the redbreasts that never came. Yesterday there was one singing cheerily in Kensington Gardens. A thrush, too, was piping now & then & the grass was as green as May. I think the climate more than anything else keeps me here. It is the best I have ever seen — at any rate the best for me, & the vapoury atmosphere is divine in its way — always luminous & always giving the distance that makes things tolerable. But I have pangs sometimes.

    Will you ask Mr Winsor if they have in the College Library Fergusson's book on Serpent Worship published by the India Office. I have two copies to dispose of & if they haven't it, shall send one of them thither.

I have no news except that my official extraterritoriality will perhaps prevent my being rector at St Andrew's, because it puts me beyond the reach of the Scottish Courts in case of malversation in office. How to rob a Scottish University suggests a serious problem. I was pleased with the election & the pleasant way it was spoken of here, though I did not want the place. Had I known what I know now, I should not have allowed myself to be put up. But I was in Paris & had forgotten among the bookstalls that I was an Excellency. I have been writing necessary notes all the morning & am tired as you see, but I shall never be tired of loving you as you deserve.

Affectionately always
Jamie.

We have to move into a new house at the end of the month. It is 31 in this same square. It is larger than this & there will be a bed for you when you come as I wish you would with all my heart & Fanny too—who is very well.

I saw Bradshaw at Cambridge the other day & we embraced over you. He is looking wonderfully well & young.

[seal of Foreign Office]

10th Dec^r, 1883.

Dear Ciarli,

I am waiting at the Foreign Office (faute d'être Ambassadeur) till the Russian Ambassador has finished boring Lord Granville He is the Baron de Mohrenheim & we call him Bohrenheim, that is, being translated, Bore 'em home, for short.

I take the occasion to say that I have written to the Duc d'Aumale in the most aggravating terms (see Bottom) enclosing your letter.

10 Lowndes Square, 6.30 p.m. Here came in Old Musurus the Turkish Ambassador, but as I had an appointment & he hadn't, I went in first — whether rightly or not Lord Granville didn't know, but thought I was right. But M. is a dear amiable old fellow & was quite content. Lord G. says the Russ is the last diplomate he knows who is like the diplomates on the stage which is very true & strictly confidential. You see how my life goes. I am wofully tired, & write this that you may know all the sooner how prompt I was in executing your commission. My letter to S. A. R. went off in half an hour after I got yours. I wrote to you the other day with a copy of du Maurier's ballad. I forgot to say (I think) that it is genuine & not a manufacture of Bromwichham. Indeed, so says internal evidence.

Affectionately yours always
Jamie.

Legation of the United States
London

20th Decr, 1883.

Dear Ciarli,

I have just received a note from the Duc d'Aumale in which, I am sorry to tell you, he says, "Sur les indications données par Mr Child j'ai non seulement fouillé mes armoires, mais consulté l'homme de France le plus compétent en ces matières, Mr Delisle, membre de l'Institut et directeur de la Biblque Natle. Il nous a été impossible de retrouver la trace du poème signalé par Mr Child." This is all he says but as he goes on to indulge me with some very kind personal assurances of &c &c & signs himself with the most "affectueux sentiments," I suppose he means to imply that he would have done what you wished had it been in his power. I shall thank him in your name accordingly.

This will come too late to wish you a merry Xmas, but in time enough to say "Happy Newyear!" perhaps. How heartily I wish you both *versteht sich.*

I suppose the Democrats will be calling me home all in good time, but in the meanwhile why couldn't you run over? Your chamber in our new house awaits you with as glad a welcome as Elmwood had to give you.

Affectionately yours
J. R. Lowell.

In the next letters, Child's incidental reference to Thackeray's 'Little Billee' barely anticipates Lowell's transmission of a copy of the ballad sent to Child by Leslie Stephen, Thackeray's son-in-law. It is interesting to observe that in a note to the 'coach and three' of 'Young Beichan' Child practically paraphrases the remarks on 'Little Billee' here expressed to Lowell.[37] And it might be added that the 'proud porter' of a later paragraph in this same letter is an echo from 'Young Beichan.'

The year 1883 marked the height of the agitation over the project for opening Shakespeare's grave. Nothing came of the project at the last, but feeling ran high on both sides, much ink was spilled, and to Child, an ocean away, the threat seemed very real.

Evangelinus Apostolides Sophocles, University Professor of Ancient, Byzantine, and Modern Greek, had died on December 17. The Harris family referred to must be that of Thaddeus William Harris, M.D. and Librarian of Harvard College. Dr Harris had died in 1856.

[37] *English and Scottish Popular Ballads*, I, 457, n. 'Little Billee' had been published, under title of 'The Three Sailors,' as long ago as 1849, in Samuel Bevan's *Sand and Canvas.*

My dear Jamie,

To think of my owing an Excellency three letters! I might say five, for I owe you two for d'Aumale. I shall think the better both of thee & of him henceforth — of thee for a true poet, and him for a true prince. Gracious as he was, I have no doubt that I have done him a favor, for I procured him two letters which he knew how to value. I am sorry that Les Visions d'Oger should be beyond finding. I shall always think that those same visions were of things to be & like True Thomas's prophecies. But the very utmost has been done, and I thank you infinitely.

I have copies of Du Maurier's ballad, but none, I think, so good as his. Had he noted where he got it, it would have been well: but some day I will write and ask him. Had it been the twentieth version I should have wanted it. By the way, I have often thought how wonderfully Thackeray hit off the ballad of low degree. There are no serious imitations, as you know, of the romantic ballad that are in the least like. It is not that they fall short, but they are fundamentally different. But Little Billee is really like the ballad fallen from its high estate. The captain of a — seventy-three!!! is a most capital stroke of genius, and I don't know a line that has more rejoyced the cockles of my heart. Well see now what was sent me for Young Beichan:

> She came to me on a horse & saddle,
> She may go back in a coach and three!

I fear the Democrats. They may yet cut their own throats, but, if you will permit me to make the remark, our President plays into their hands by interceding for concessions[?] under their compulsion. A politician never dares do the thing that would make him. We need not fear the Democrats, if we would act with independence about silver money, civil-service and the Irish. —

You have given more satisfaction to your countryman than any minister I have lived to see. I wish you could have heard my brother in law Butler (former senior partner to Evarts) speak of our minister on Christmas Day. Every honor that you get is felt as an honor done. — Now I have a thing on my mind that I want you to do. The recent talk of violating Shakspere's grave has caused a strong feeling in America. We don't want his bones to be threatened, as they will be as long as the rector of Stratford may any day give permission to dig the dust enclosed there. If he would win a curse that stirs those stones, so he shall win a blessing that secures the everlasting immunity of them. I don't know how the interference and prohibition could be conducted. Parliament has all power, I suppose. Lord Granville could tell you. Matthew Arnold is now too far off to be reached by voice. Had I thought in time I would have urged him to join with you in getting in motion a petition or what not for the perpetual inviolability of Shakspere's bones. — If you think well of such a step, I would undertake a memorial to be signed by everybody this side of the water: but I should not want America to take the pas of England. It would be best to have a paper drawn up in England and signed over here. But first one needs to know what is feasible, then the best way of going to work. I feel sure that you will want something effectual done. Do think and talk the matter over, will you, and let me know your conclusion.

I cannot come to that gîte in your new house. I must keep at my pund o tow. But your twice mentioning it gives me almost a feeling of having been there, and of your sending me back in your coach & three. (Wasn't I afraid of your proud porter!)

I suppose you have seen Sophocles's death noticed. I shall miss him very much. He was himself to the last. He made a generous provision for Dr Harris's family, and left the rest of his money to our Library for Greek books — but in the name of the uncle that educated him, not his own

Eady (if that's his spelling) [88] wrote me that he would send back the Campbell MSS in the diplomatic pouch. I had determined not to do this, but am so nervous about their being meddled with at the Custom House, and so fearful of the express here not *paying through*, that I now will beg you just to let them come to the Legation, & have them sent to Ellis & White, 29 New Bond St. I can rely upon E. & W. paying all expenses to Berwickshire.

I was charmed to have you wandering about the book-stalls of Paris. This very day I received your Romania for October. It always seems to come direct from you.

I am now within a very short time of your New Year. So Heaven keep & bless you, & bring you back in due time. We want you here but need you there, and since you are happy here's to a respectable new President! Love and New Year's wishes to Mrs Lowell, and thanks once more for all you have done.

Ever your affectionate

Ciarli

James Russell Lowell, Esq.
London

31, Lowndes Square.
S. W.

17th January, 1884.

Dear Ciarli,

I was going to write to you today — your delightful letter wouldn't let me rest. But alas, the Atlantic Cable is the *trouble-fête* of diplomatists. I have just got a cypher telegram which I can't read here because the key is at the Legation & I must hasten thither to find out what I am to do. So I barely enclose my love & a copy of "Little Billee" which Stephen sent me for you. It may interest you & perhaps be of use to you, for it seems to be

[88] I.e., Adee.

63

the first draught — but seems also (to me, at least) a less sprightly running than the last. I remember a variant which Thackeray used to sing in select circles in which little Billee's terror is expressed more graphically by the verse

"Into his trowsers he did p—"

but you can hardly use it.

Goodbye.

Your affectionate
Jamie.

The birthday letter of 1884 reflects the heated controversy over the teaching of the classical languages, and more particularly of Greek, which had reached a Cambridge peak in the Phi Beta Kappa address, 'A College Fetish,' by Charles Francis Adams at the Harvard Commencement of 1883. Actually, Adams's valuation of Plato in the matter of hiccoughs had been borrowed from a letter of his great-grandfather written to Thomas Jefferson.

Feb 22, 1884.

Dearest Jamie,

I have had to keep the day through continuous work, till now past four, and could make no other holiday than wishing you well unusually much and often.

I hope some sort of festival may have been held in London. Mrs Lowell has her way of honoring the day of course. Perhaps you write verses every twenty second of February, and show yourself invulnerable to time. Your last letters have the full sound of youth, youth without greenhed, as Chaucer says, but green youth still. I always thought you maintained the tide of life at perfect fulness with no sign of an ebb. When you began to complain of gout in the thorax I had a fear that a turn was coming. But no — you needed only a larger sphere. You were a little cramped, and your verge being widened so that you could draw a full breath, you were the same ambrosial being that you ever had been And that I see you continue to be. Wherefore another birthday is no loss. How much good life you have had the last year, and how much you have amassed for years to come. You are to have at least one more year in England, and I shall give my voice for any President whose policy it shall be to keep you where you wish to be.

Add to your glories this year the securing of Shakspere's everlasting rest. Don't let that consummation be hazarded. I want you to have a chief hand in bringing it about.

I can tell you, we need you here now. The chemists are in conspiracy to oust Greek, and then Latin; and would have us claver[?] with learned[?] fellows who can only analyse coaltar. They want to cut loose from the old world completely. Charles Adams has persuaded them that there is nothing to be found in Plato but the art of stopping hiccough. Our President's dogma is that a man is "liberally educated" who knows any one thing well and can use his own language — that is, write intelligibly! This will not be your doctrine when you speak to the Scotch students.

The bells are ringing their third & last peal for Washington & you. Benedicite for another year. Love to Mrs Lowell.

Ever your affectionate
Ciarli.

In the spring of 1884 two tercentenary celebrations claimed the presence of the American Minister, that of the University of Edinburgh in April, where he received his fourth honorary degree, and Emmanuel College, Cambridge, in June, where he was the guest of honor at the commemoration banquet, though the principal speaker was Charles Eliot Norton, official delegate from John Harvard's university to John Harvard's college. With four gowns, Lowell remarked, he should be able to keep himself warm 'without Harvard.'[39] Actually both Child and he were made LL.D. at the Harvard Commencement of this year, as becomes apparent in subsequent letters of Child's.

Legation of the United States
London

9th April, 1884.

Dear Ciarli,

do, please come over & go with me to Emmanuel (Don't take me for a captain in the Salvation Army). Come straight to my house, 31 Lowndes Square) & we will rejoice together. I have just accepted an invitation from the Master & Fellows.

I say this provided I get back from Edinbro' alive. Thither I go next Monday, & such a round of speechifying & junketting as they have in preparation was never heard of on this planet. It is as if all the 4th July's from the first were rolled into one as Dante proposed with the two planets. I write in great haste just to say that I will never forgive you if you don't come, but shall love you always whether you come or not.

Affectionately yours
J. R. L.

By April of 1884 the tensions of one of the most fiercely fought presidential campaigns in American history were mounting. Child was

---

[39] Letter to George Putnam, 8 April 1884 (*Letters of James Russell Lowell*, III, 111). Lowell's third honorary degree, also in this year, had been from St Andrews.

then thinking of a Republican victory, and of President Arthur or Senator George F. Edmunds, of Vermont, the reform candidate, as the 'lucky Jerry.' Yet it was Blaine who actually received the Republican nomination in June.

Child had to wait another ten years for the Sharpe ballads. They were finally sold in 1893 to Child's indefatigable friend, William Macmath of Edinburgh, who promptly copied out transcripts for Child in his own hand.[40]

April 27 [1884]

Things impossible are all the more to be believed, my dear Jamie, sed de rebus faciendis eadem non est ratio! — Why do you tantalise me by saying come, and we will rejoice together, when I can't any way come. If you asked Vincentius Bellovacensis to drop his Speculum Historiale just as his vacation was coming, or his trentals all sung, his novices all schooled & swinged, his pen fresh nibbed and his parchment spread, what would Vinc Bell answer? — I can conceive of nothing more precious than to go to Emmanuel with you and talk it over afterwards at Lowndes Sq, but all the three fates are against it — Atropos, because I have not the time to turn about in — Lachesis, because I lack æs, and Clotho because I have not wedding garments. The big, invincible reason of all is that I can work in vacation and can do little in term. Just to go & come in a month, I am too old for, and if I used my month so I could not give a fortnight to my family, as promised, or go on a pilgrimage to Stockbridge, now a village of the dead, as I have vowed. I say nothing of 300 roses which are to bloom in June–July, or of other trivial reasons. (Mrs Lowell will think that not so very bad, and it would not be were not seeing you in question.)

The democrats are so maddened by the gods that I think we shall have a Republican President and that means your staying for years more — I know it. Perhaps Arthurus praeses nunc, erit praeses futurus. Ex contrario erit Edmundus fortasse Ieremias jucundus, or the lucky Jerry. But any decent president will go on his knees to you to stay, and since the life keeps you young & makes you happy, you adorn it, & we the people profit thereby. I must wish against wish. —

Sir Hugh Campbell wrote me two or three days since that he had received back his volumes "with a most courteous note from your minister". Thrice kind of you. No note was rigorously required, but he will think the better of me ever after on account of your note. My mind is much easier for the things being on the right side of the water. I know of only one more parcel of ballads to get, & these were among the papers of Charles Kirkpatrick Sharpe. Mr Allardyce, who is writing Sharpe's life, has them and by and by I think he will concede a copy to me. I am in relations with him. Percy's

[40] As explained in the advertisement to Part IX of the *Ballads*.

66

collections, or sweepings of his study, are to be sold the coming 29th and the college will buy all that is worth anything, unless something goes wrong. I imagine that there is little or nothing in the way of ballads which would concern anything but a general gatherum like mine.

Man to call —

P.S. *He staid from 4 to 10!* Equa manu pulsant professorum tuguria legatorumque turres.[41] Farewell with a million of thanks & love

Ciarli

In the next letter, in opposing Cleveland to Blaine, Child was anticipating, for the Democratic convention had not yet assembled. Cleveland was nominated July 11.

Richard Claverhouse Jebb, the editor of Sophocles, was another recipient of an honorary degree at the Harvard Commencement of 1884, along with Child and Lowell.

Cambridge,
July 1. [1884]

My dear Jamie,

The ocean cable has been really useful of late, by giving rather frequent reports of you. I have been wondering whether gout would ever come again, and was ready to insure you in any office. I hope it is a gout serene, and not one of the grander sort, and that it will be under subjection long ere this comes. If it be of the higher style, I know that even the thought that somebody was writing you a letter would give you a twinge: the contact is too close. There is comfort in the thought that, once through, you can't collect enough argols, red[?] bile, or whatever the secretion be, for another bout till near the end of Cleveland's (Blaine's?) administration. I do not mean to speak with that levity which the unexperienced think the proper tone for such cases. Et in arthritide ego! I wish the news had come by letter rather than by telegraph, so that I might think of the crisis as well over already.

I know that you have seen Charles Norton and the cable again tells us that you produced a marked effect on the dons at Cambridge. I am now to tell you that you were a very prominent interest of *our* commencement. The President insisted that I should say something at the dinner. It was in vain for me to writhe: he would have it so. He told me that I was to have a degree, *with you*, and must say a word for you. I was thoroughly wretched at the prospect of being called upon. I know I shall never be able to make a speech. The arena swims before me and the inhuman shouts or

---

[41] Cf. Horace, *Odes*, I, 4:

Pallida Mors aequo pulsat pede pauperum tabernas
regumque turres.

claps of the wretches who sit safe around only complete the paralysis of my mind. The President said something very good about you when he conferred the degree. I begged him to send me the words for transmission, but he has forgotten or neglected to do so. An allusion to you by Jebb was warmly received at the dinner, and another to our *beloved* Lowell by Lodge. I am ashamed to confess to you that I could say almost nothing, even with you for a theme (and what I said got badly deranged in reporting: here it is.) [42]

Mr. President and Gentlemen, — It was conceded, for reasons pertaining to the general advantage, that if the president of the alumni should chance to lay his hand on my shoulder and pronounce the awful words, "You're wanted," a simply formal response should suffice. It was indeed intimated to me that if I could not say anything for myself, I might say a word or two for Mr. Lowell. It could not but be a great pleasure to me to be associated with Mr Lowell, in any way, and however accidentally. I will say that all the admiration and applause which have fallen to him in these half dozen years of his absence and which we at home have been so happy to see him win, would fail to give him a cordial satisfaction, would play round his head and not come to his heart, unless he were assured of the continued attachment of his fellow-students, as well as of their approbation and that of his countrymen. I believe that all present will be ready to give him that assurance in full measure.

I shall send you Part II of Ballads this week, I suppose. I have no manuscript ballads to get hold of now but a parcel of Kirkpatrick Sharpe's. We got everything that Bishop Percy had accumulated for a 4th volume of the Reliques. A drefful poor volume it would have been. Among all the papers there are not eight or ten traditional ballads. Having been gathered about 1775, or earlier, they ought to be a good deal better. But ballads should have been collected as early as 1600; then there would have been such a nice crop; the aftermath is very weedy. —

People hereabout doubt whether we can beat Blaine. We all wait anxiously for the Democratic nomination. Your friends Charles Saunders & Chapman have reluctantly decided to support Blaine (won't that bring Cambridge back to you! — and Alfred Wood has retired from business, & Wm Kimball, who of late seemed to do none.) Best love to Mrs Lowell. Ever your faithful & affectionate

Ciarli

Cambridge, July 24. [1884]

Dearest Jamie,

Eliot sent me your laudes, which may be nothing to what you get over there, but will have a home-felt flavor.

[42] At this point Child has pasted to the letter clippings of his remarks and of parts of the remarks by Jebb and Lodge, taken from the *Boston Advertiser* of 26 June 1884. The clipping of his own remarks he has emended heavily in pen-and-ink; a transcription of the emended version follows in the text.

I sent you Part II the other day, not expecting that you would have in the height of the season more than a minute to give to it. Look at Tam Lin, if anything: that or Young Beichan is as good as any for a specimen.

Edwin Abbot, a Harvard College man, who has done me kind services of much importance, (tried to improve the state of my dilapidated investments) asked me to give him letters to my friends in England. He is coming over for a month or two of rest, being a hard-worked Railway man. I told him that I had hardly a friend in England. I could think only of Sara Darwin, & ventured also on our Glasgow man. He wants to see the Universities & Westminster especially. I don't know that you can help him by any ambassadorial recommendation. You will be engaged, I know, from night to morning. But not to fail to do the utmost I could for a true friend, I shall write a line to you, and if you can help him to what he wants in any way (possibly you can get him a better view of the Tower than he would have with a mob) I know you will.

Having to go to Boston today, I tore out an article from an old North American and soon saw that I had you in hand. Nothing so pleasant have I read for years. Your affectionate

F. Ciarli

I tell Abbot how devoured you are

Lowell's supposition in his Christmas note of 1884 was correct: he was supplanted as Minister in the early spring of 1885 by Edward J. Phelps, Vermont lawyer and Democrat.

The good report of Mrs Lowell was the last. Exactly two months later death closed her long course of suffering that had begun in Spain nearly six years before.

Legation of the United States
London

19th Dec: 1884.

Dear Ciarli,

I saw in the Daily News tother day a quotation from another version of the Du Maurier ballad I sent you. I at once wrote to the editor asking for a copy to be sent to you. I have just received & enclose it.

I have time only for these few lines. A couple of hundred diplomas of the Birmingham & Midland Institute await my signature. I have already signed about seven hundred. I wish they were banknotes for £1000 each which we were to divide between us! But my autograph is *not yet* worth quite so much.

I don't know yet whether I am coming home or not, but suppose that Democratic notions of Civil Service Reform will require my recall.

Fanny is *very* well & would send her love were she here. I wish you a Merry Xmas & Happy New Year with all my heart.

Affectionately yours

Jamie.

F. J. Child, Esq.

Feb 19, 1885

Dearest Jamie

We have known for two days that we must soon hear what now we have heard. Before that I had thought that all was well.

I feel now as if you must be alone in another sense than if you were here, but this is perhaps only our own feeling reflected upon you. Surely a thousand hearts are feeling for you there as here; surely among those there are those who are deeply attached to you; and surely neither there nor here is there any immediate consolation. My only comfort in your case is still a great one. Were you without any belief, and were I without any belief, this winter day would be summer compared with my thoughts, this sinking sun high noon. You believe, you *know*; you will help others more than they can help you. Sympathy can only make this day darker if it means fellow[?] grief that all is over. Love, if it can perish, only makes us more forlorn. You have never thought so, you have never sung that; such despair will never have your voice or your assent.

We were very much troubled about your future before, seeing no way to our wishes; but this was not among my apprehensions. Our love will attend anxiously upon you, now & henceforth. Ever your most affectionate

Ciarli

February 22 [1885]

Dearest Jamie

I was looking forward with pleasure to writing to you today: the only question was whether to write a greeting to *arrive* on the 22d. I am very glad to have been saved from that. Considering how short our term is, and with what mortal misgivings our best hopes are mixed, even a birth-day under the happiest circumstances is shaded with a thought. You have loved this world and have known how to get the happiness out of it. I know by my own exquisite pleasure in seeing the crocuses and columbines shoot, and hailing the first robin, that yours must be too sweet to relinquish or to have her whom you love relinquish. For myself, if not subject to decay of body & mind, I could see a thousand changes of the seasons with undiminishing delight. I am now looking forward to one more, but alas, count those that at best can be left. Another life must be better than this. So far as nature goes — with those that lead a tranquil rural life — one hardly wants a

70

better. But indeed most men sadly need life to be bettered. Another life is to be better even than this was for you when your rich hair was all of one tint. Credo quia impossibile est. This often used to be my thought: it has not entered into man's heart to conceive what is preparing; a life to which this is exile; a delight beyond all that poetry, roses, skies can give; and this is not strange, it is the simplest thing in the world; this is what we have been all along saying when we called God infinitely good & loving, not knowing what the words meant: the power that can do for us beyond what we ask or think. It is a necessity as plain as mathematics. And all that have breathed are to come to this. Another impossibility that must be. This or nothing: and who that is not blinded and deafened by misery or grief believes that the insubstantial pageant is to dissolve & fade? What, the man that wrote those words ? or better, the man that suffered on the cross ? or the sweet pure souls we have known?

I don't know how to think of you. I have never seen you when grief was fresh. But I have a kind of confidence, not in the strength of your spirit, but in the clearness of your vision. I believe that you believe the things you have sung, and your kind. Wort gehalten wird in jenen Räumen is one of the sayings that has given me most solace. And as for another — nur so lang sie liebten, waren sie. I want no better assurance of deathlessness. — I am writing, as I feel, dearest Jamie, and not writing at you. Your loneliness oppresses my thoughts dreadfully. I hope you have some very tender friends as well as admirers there. I know you must have. Ever your faithful affectionate

Ciarli

Legation of the United States
London

16th April, 1885.

Dear Ciarli,

your letter was very sweet & dear to me & all the more that Fanny was always fond of you & often spoke of you with affection. You were one of the friends whom we looked forward to meeting with most pleasure. As it is. I look forward to nothing. She was planning a rivalry with you in roses & meant to have her garden prettier than ever. The last walk I took with her (on the Sunday before she was taken ill) the shrubs in Kensington Gardens were some of them giving hints of Spring & she spoke of trying whether they would not stand our climate. She was always planning about her garden. And now the Spring has come & she who gave it all its sweetness will never come again. But she is surely with God, for never was there a soul readier for him or that would have been more welcome. She was nobly religious, as she was noble in all things. A more beautiful nature, so rare a mixture of strength & sweetness, never was known to me.

I have taken my passage by the *Scythia* which sails for Boston on the 10th of June. I would come sooner if I could, but am not yet quite sure when my successor will arrive. I shall have to stay & coach him a little. I am glad to hear excellent accounts of him & feel quite sure that he will be acceptable here. I think I am glad to be relieved. I look forward to seeing my old haunts again with a poignant pathos.

Goodbye & God bless you till I take you by the hand.

Always your affectionate

Jami.

Professor Child.

With Lowell's return to America there was less reason for correspondence with such a Cambridge friend as Child. Yet Lowell did not go back to Elmwood at once; it was rented, and for him too full of painful memories. He lived at first with his daughter, Mrs Burnett, in Southborough, or, for shorter stretches, with his sister, Mrs Putnam, at 68 Beacon Street, Boston. And he went abroad each spring and summer for the four successive years 1886–89, returning finally to Elmwood in November of 1889, with less than two years to live.

Yet he must have been often in Cambridge before that. He did not become Smith Professor Emeritus until Commencement 1886, reading Dante in a seminar for some weeks the preceding winter, and was an Overseer of the College from 1887 until his death.

In any case, after a gap of nearly two years, the correspondence resumes with Lowell's thank-you note for a copy of *The Child of Bristowe*, printed by Child in his modernized version for Christmas 1886. The copy given Lowell has not been traced, but there is in the Harvard Library a copy bound, in colored and blind-tooled leather, by Miss Emily Tuckerman, the 'Young Lady' of the *Scholar's Letters* published in 1920. This copy, which has bound with it Child's *Debate of the Body and Soul*, 1888 (inscribed by Child to Miss Tuckerman), was bequeathed by Miss Tuckerman to the Child Memorial Library.

Deerfoot Farm,
Southborough, Mass.

Dear Ciarli,   27th Dec: 1886.

thanks thick & threefold for your delightful little Xmas-gift. It is all the sweeter to me that you recited parts of it to me once. There never was a better Child than he of Bristowe but one, & I know where he lives, though *you* don't.

I enclose in return the lease of my love renewed for another year & all loving wishes for your happiness during ever so many more. With love to Mrs Child,

Affectionately yours
J. R. Lowell.

F. J. Child, Esq.

Deerfoot Farm,
Southborough, Mass.
11th Jan: 1887.

Dear Ciarli,

I shipped to you this morning by express two boxes of cigars which I hope will reach you safely. One is for you & one for Grace, which latter I beg you to deliver with my love. Of course they won't turn out so good as I said they were (such is the perverse nature of things) — but with your lips to help 'em they ought to be tolerable company.

Affectionately yours
J. R. L.

Professor Child.

With Lowell in England in the spring of 1887, Child wrote to support the plea of the Furnesses, father and son, that Lowell present a poem at the centennial celebration of the United States Constitution to be held in Philadelphia the following September. The younger Furness was then a student at Harvard, preparatory to following his father in the Shakespeare *Variorum*. The plea, as Lowell's reply shows, was unavailing, in spite of Child's telling quotation from the beautiful *romance* of Conde Arnaldos. At the memorial exercises in Independence Hall, on September 17, a new national hymn was recited by Francis Marion Crawford.

Sara Sedgwick, it will be remembered, had married William Darwin, son of Charles.[43] The ballad 'Adam Bell, Clim of the Clough, and William of Cloudsley' appears in Part V of the *Ballads*, published in the spring of 1888.

Cambridge, May 17,
1887

Dearest Jamie

By the way in which William & Sara Darwin are enjoying May, one would think that you could not have changed skies to advantage. We never had such a May, and we want a poet to express our delight. It is to the June

[43] See Child's Christmas letter of 1877.

you have sung as a squash before it is a peascod. I have been limping and himping about among my rose-bushes, a Vulcan with 400 Venuses, but no Mars as yet, though 4000 Mars are coming. I shall never be free to go to Europe or to go anywhere if I keep on so, and at last cold wisdom has conquered superfluous folly, and I have taken out Adam Bell to polish him up for court. But before I go to work I must keep word with Horace Furness, who, as well as his father, has written to you, to entreat a poem from you for next September. The occasion is of course a very great one, and were you this side of the lake I think you would be persuaded. I had some remorse, bethinking myself how you went away tired with lectures, and how all birds had a right to sing for themselves, or for the folks of their own tree, in summer. Tal respuesta le fué à dar: Yo no digo esta cancion sino à quien conmigo va! And you don't want S. P. Q. A. at your heels in summer. But when I think that you have solely sovereign[?] sung and are the dean[?] among our poets, it seems as great a lack to have you away from such a ceremony as Cleveland himself. *You* would be the man of the occasion, and the nation, not merely a rabble of Congressmen, will be present. You would do what I most of all things wish, make yourself known, in your person I mean, to West & South; you would say something which would improve the Constitution's chance of getting through another hundred years; the occasion would be equally good for your name & credit and for patriotism and good government. I feel this very strongly, but will not preach from the text. (Furness intimated to me, what he did not wish to say to you, that your expenses would be paid to & fro.) Clearly your concession would be a great sacrifice. Everybody (except politicians) would feel that. If you can make the sacrifice, you shall never be asked to make such another (I speak for the 50 millions.) When I think what unspeakable service such verses as yours about Virginia, spoken before the nation, would do, I feel that you had better consent even if death were the price to you. But it would not be. You would be stronger and happier for a score of years to come. You shall not be obliged to read more. I hope you are well and young.

Ever your loving
F. Ciarli.

Hon. James Russell Lowell, London.

2, Radnor Place,
Hyde Park. W.
16th June, 1887.

Dearest Ciarli,

Surely I would if I could, but they hurry me so that I can't find out my own mind. I have done so many involuntaries that I have little left to say, but I had begun to see my way to something when they beset me & upset me with telegrams — so I said *"no!"* Who can hold counsel with the Muse when he feels that the cable is laying wait for him & may give him an electric

74

shock at any minute — "how are you getting on? have you begun it yet?" & the Devil knows what. Other men may have composure under such a harrow, but I am a poor toad.

I think of you in your Rose-garden, my dear Saadi, with a longing love. You went near my heart with your quotation from my favourite Conde Arnaldos. 'Tis the best lecture on the *Ars Poetica* known to me. But quien hubiese tal ventura? Not I with the Constitution, which is by no means the cancion *he* was blessed with hearing.

This is my tenth epistle today & I am tired. But you will know that all the paper I leave blank wouldn't hold the affection I feel for you.

Always your loving
Jamie.

F. J. Child, Esq.

Lowell was still in England when he wrote the following note on behalf of Phillips Smalley, son of his close friend George Washburn Smalley, the noted journalist and war correspondent, who had been living in England for many years as European representative of the *New York Tribune*.

2, Radnor Place,
Hyde Park. W.
9th Sept. 1887.

Dear Ciarli,

be kind to Phillips Smalley for my sake & you will be kind to me. He is going to enter the Harvard Law School &, never having been separated from his own people before, will be as lonely as Mungo Park in Africa. Be as good to him as the black women were to the Scot, though not for the same reason — since he will find plenty of ways to have his corns ground in a new country.

Affectionately yours
J. R. Lowell.

Professor Child.

We come now to the last interchange. Lowell was nearing the date, April 13, of his address before the Reform Club of New York, on 'The Place of the Independent in Politics,' and had apparently sought Child's help in selecting an appropriate passage from *The Advancement of Learning* for quotation. The 'little book,' a copy of W. A. Wright's edition, 1880, is in the Harvard Library, with Child's stars at all the passages mentioned. The volume, apparently returned after all by Lowell, was presented to the Library by Child's daughter, Mrs Scoggin.

Lowell actually used the first of the marked passages, '12 (3),' in his address.

In rendering thanks for the just published *Heartsease and Rue*, Child is the true *amicus musarum*, appreciating his poet-friend to the last. The copy given Child came to the Harvard Library with the other gifts of Mrs Scoggin, and has duly pasted in the slip cut from Lowell's note of March 26, with the inscription 'To F. J. Child with the love of J. R. L. 7th March, 1888.' It is interesting to note that the presentation copies to Norton, Thomas Wentworth Higginson, and Thomas Bailey Aldrich, at Harvard, are all dated March 7.

To the list of poems in *Heartsease and Rue* (including, by implication, ' "Franciscus de Verulamio sic cogitavit" ') Child adds the still later 'Turner's Old Téméraire,' which made its first appearance in the April 1888 *Atlantic*, and was included by Norton in the posthumous *Last Poems*, 1895. Child alludes also to other current literary activities, such as the introduction to a new edition of Walton's *Angler*, published by Little Brown in 1889, which is one of Lowell's finest essays. On other evidence, the introduction for *The History of the World's Progress*, inserted in the second edition of 1888, should have been written in the winter of 1886–87,[44] but perhaps Lowell had not yet finished it.

March 24. [1888]

Dearest Jamie,

I don't hear of your coming this way, and suppose you resolutely set to write your preface to Walton's Angler, and perhaps to The World's Progress, or whatever that other book may be. I note, after writing my date, that we are nigh the end of the month, and remember that you were to make the speech in New York, and that I was to send you a passage in Bacon's Advancement, quomodo cogitavit F. B. de V. There are two or three passages, as to which I would have you refresh your recollection, and you will do so more handily if I send the little book (which I do not wish to have returned.) I have starred some of the best, on pp. 12(3), 16(8), 19(2), 22(6), 40(6), 73(7). The one I had most in mind was 16(8). But they are all noble or charming, and so are many more. What can be more felicitous than his last paragraph 73(7)?

You have not yet had my thanks for Heartsease & Rue. I could not read it through at a sitting, like Calverley's rhymes. I have read most of it aloud,

[44] Letters to Charles Eliot Norton, 24 December 1886, and Grace Norton, 3 January 1887 (*Letters of James Russell Lowell*, III, 171, 176); letter to Henry James (*New Letters*, p. 296).

and much of it more than once. Not only will it bear reading more than once, but one reading — unless the reader be quicker far than I — will never take in the beauty of either thought or phrase. It seems to me that this must be your best book, though I am aware that of good things the last is apt to seem best. I am not sure that I could say what I like best, even of these last. Some things in Agassiz, some things in G. Curtis, some things in Endymion, E. G. de R., Phoebe!!, Burning of Letters, Foreboding, The Lesson!!, Sea Shell, Credidimus J. r., In an Album: that is not quite all the volume after all. The Téméraire follows, not inferior to any. Should you (over God's forbod!) make no more volumes, this would be a good ending. Amen, par charite, god beginning maketh god ending, quoth Hendyng. Hoping that you are blither than when I last saw you, ever your loving

Ciarli

Lowell's rejoinder thanks Child in turn for his recent gift, a copy of the privately printed *Debate of the Body and Soul* which Child had modernized from one of the Middle English versions printed by Thomas Wright in his edition of Walter Map, Camden Society, 1841. As in the case of *The Child of Bristowe*, the copy given Lowell has not come to light, but, as was pointed out in connection with the gift of that earlier opusculum, a copy bound with *The Child* by Miss Tuckerman is in the Harvard Library.[45] Lowell had shown his familiarity with Walter Map or Mapes, of Goliardic fame, when in 1885 he wrote to William D. Howells, president of the newly formed Tavern Club in Boston, assenting to his election as an honorary member, and quoting the four lines beginning 'Meum est propositum in taberna mori.' These lines were adopted and are still used as the Tavern Club song.[46]

The first pages of this letter and of Child's of the next day (Child's last letter) are reproduced in Plate VIII, from the originals at Harvard.

Deerfoot Farm,
26th March, 1888.

Dearest Ciarli,

a thousand thanks for your letter & for the book. I had already acted on your hint & had what I thought the fittest passage copied for me, but am glad to enrich my little library here with the A. of L. as my Bacon is at Elmwood.

I am glad you find something to like in my book for I love to please you.

[45] See Lowell's note to Child of 27 December 1886.

[46] M. A. DeWolfe Howe, *A Partial (and Not Impartial) Semi-Centennial History of the Tavern Club 1884–1934* (Boston, 1934), pp. 40–41.

Nothing is ever so good as it should be (except a rose now & then) — it is so hard to make anything right, & one is apt to despair too soon.

This reminds me that I have never thanked you for *your* little book which pleased me more than I can say. I happened to have Walter Mapes here & could therefore compare as I read. I think you have shown wonderful seamanship in hitting the channel (& on a leeshore too, as such things always are) between the bristling reef of archaism & the mudflats of newspaper-English. I had quite forgotten how good the poem was.

I write something on the opposite leaf for you to paste into your book.

Affectionately yours
J. R. Lowell.

Professor Child.

March 27. [1888]

Dearest Jamie,

Yours of yesterday having just come to hand (I didn't mean to have you write — the friend that makes us write notes is but little less bad than the one that makes us sign them) I can't help finishing an incomplete stanza which I find in your shame-fast disclaimer:

> "Nothing is good as it should be —
> 'Cept now and then a rose" —
> And now & then your poetry —
> And now & then your prose

(And mostly, women, as witness your verses. I thought I had known almost as many perfections as anybody, but now I see that my world has been small.)

To think that some youngster will presently send your book to a girl, and tell her that she will find his case pretty well, but imperfectly, hit off in the Seashell!

I was telling you what I liked best, not what I liked. "Find *something* to like" indeed!

Ever your most affectionate
F. C.

Lowell's 'crossing into the seventies' was celebrated by one of the most distinguished of Tavern Club dinners. The Club archives show that Child was forced to decline an invitation to attend, because of 'an unfavorable state of health.' His greeting to Lowell, apparently not preserved, brought the following response.

68 Beacon Street,
23rd Feb: 1889.

Dearest Ciarli,

whatever you do is well done &, whether your accidents were at the dinner or not, I knew that your real presence was there in love & good wishes. I feel no sensible change in crossing into the seventies — least of all could I have expected to find any in the warmth of my affection for you. I shall look for a little more deference on the part of youngsters like you after this my promotion, but shall try not to be uppish. Hoping to see you soon — & the wish is partly selfish for it always does me good,

Affectionately yours
J. R. Lowell.

Professor Child.

Lowell's return to Elmwood in the autumn of 1889, after an absence of more than ten years, reduced still further the occasion for letters between the two friends. There remain three brief notes from Lowell, which are given below, but of the late meetings face to face, and of the final parting, we should know nothing but for the *Scholar's Letters to a Young Lady*. The correspondence of the scholar-friends is therefore concluded with a series of passages relating to Lowell taken bodily from Child's letters to his younger correspondent.[47] The three notes from Lowell himself have been interspersed according to date.

The 'first severe illness' of Lowell's life, as he called it,[48] occurred in the spring of 1890, when he was confined to his bed for six weeks, attended by his old friend Morrill Wyman. This was the true beginning of the end, for he never really recovered, though the final end did not come until 12 August 1891. We learn from incidental references in the *Letters to a Young Lady* that during these last months Child paid regular visits to Elmwood, often covering the four miles from Kirkland Street and return on foot. Child's own death took place just five years later, on 11 September 1896, with his great work all but finished.

Tuesday, 12th November, 1889.

. . . In the afternoon James Lowell looked in, and now that he is established at Elmwood I shall see him often as of old — which makes the world look more friendly. Who says that literature is ill-paid? He had written a little poem, a very short one, I think, not to order, but for his own amuse-

[47] Reprinted with the kind permission of the Atlantic Company (formerly the Atlantic Monthly Press), publishers of the *Scholar's Letters*.
[48] Scudder, *James Russell Lowell*, II, 397.

79

ment, or perhaps because he could not help. A newspaper sends him a thousand dollars and asks only that he will send *something*, and he sends off his little poem. Going back to the house where he used to be happy makes him grave. His daughter is with him and has changed things just enough to have them not too familiar. . . .

Friday, 14 *March*, 1890.

. . . Nothing has happened. The only thing we have to think of is James Lowell. I saw him this morning. This day makes three weeks in bed for him. He looks white, and very noble, I think. Our good doctor, who is close upon 80, spent two nights with him. I saw him, and he speaks with some comfort of the case. Still there is no security though J. L. is much more comfortable. The doctor speaks with admiration of L.'s courage and serenity. He must live. He reads light things, and he told me this morning that he had both heard and seen the robins, from his bed. I, who have been out every day, have seen no robin. They come to him first, and he has eyes which see many things that come late to me, or not at all. Life would be much grayer without J. L. . . .

Sunday, May 11, 1890.

. . . Harry James wrote to Grace Norton the other day expressing the most earnest wish that Lowell would never show himself in London in a state of declining health. The glittering society would no more mind him than a cavalry man minds the friend that lies in his way. So I gathered from what H. J. said: the cavalry man would, I fancy, if he could, so I apologize to him, and H. J. did not bring him in. But what a world! Who cares for its flattery or its fondling then? . . .

Leslie Stephen, an intimate friend of Lowell's English years, who had visited Elmwood as early as 1863, spent several weeks there in the summer of 1890, at the same time receiving an honorary degree at the Harvard Commencement. This was Thomas Wentworth Higginson's first summer in Dublin, New Hampshire, which was to be his summer headquarters for the rest of his life.

Elmwood,
Cambridge, Mass.

20th June, 1890.

Dear Ciarli,

when I proposed to myself the rather desperate venture of having some people to meet Stephen at dinner tonight I naturally wanted you among the first if not sooner. But I heard you were abed with gout & so didn't trouble you with a note. When it was too late I heard you were *ingambe* again.

80

Now T. W. H. whom I had asked is in Dublin & can't come, & I wish you to take the place originally meant for you. I want you very much. At 7 o'clock.

Affectionately yours
J. R. Lowell.

Professor Child

Elmwood,
Cambridge, Mass.

1st July, 1890.

Dear Ciarli,

come dine with me & be my love on Thursday at 1/2 past seven. Morning dress for the greater ease of all concerned.

Affectionately yours
J. R. Lowell.

F. J. C.

Wednesday, 23rd October, 1889 [i.e., 1890?], 6 P.M.

. . . I found J[ames] L[owell] downstairs, and he staid below all the afternoon. He looked haggard, I must own. . . . There are two comfortable signs of his mending: he had come back to a pipe and he liked to talk of old Boston. How he, being a Cambridge boy, should know the wharves, as I, born close to salt water, I don't know. I found that he used to board the East Indiamen (for we had ships in plenty then) and they would give him rattans and fishing-poles (bamboos). But I thought he would not come up to me on one point: "Did you ever lick molasses on the wharves?" "Yes, and go in from Cambridge to do it!"

Now I have materials for his biography which no other man can possess. — Well, though he had not regained his strength, he was like himself, and I was greatly comforted. . . .

Then Lowell's last note to Child — from 'the modern Job.'

Elmwood,
Cambridge.

18th March, 1891.

Carissimo Ciarli,

haud ignarus mali, I learn, if not to succor, at least to sympathize. I had a sharp bout of it, but the enemy is now in full retreat. I shudder to think of you clattering over to College on crutches. You must be careful. A coax, I think, would be more suitable to your needs & to your dignity. I am far beyond any need of them. I could dance, I could caper, were it not that I

81

have another bother which disables me. Wyman says it's of no consequence, but, like poverty it is d—d inconvenient. Old Age is forgetful & leaves doors ajar through which all the maladies Caliban invoked on Prospero have taken the chance to slip in upon me. But in every other way I feel the better for my gout.

The moment I get rid of this, I shall come to collogue with you. I sent back your frame this afternoon. It was a great medicine.

Tuo affettuosissimo
Il Giobbe moderno.

F. J. C.

August 4, 1891.

. . . You hope that J. L. may be better. I fear that there is no hope of anything but a short rally, and the hope of that is but slight. I think much of my parting with him the day before I went to Stockbridge. It was very possible that something might happen; still I really expected to find him in his study again. He was put to bed — and he does not like a bed — three or four days after, and it is most doubtful whether he will ever leave it. His good-bye sounded sad that Friday. I assumed a cheerfulness which I did not feel. . . . When he goes he will take off a great cantle of my world. He has been a good friend for many years and always *hold und treu*. And a very good man too, simple, faithful, with a nobleness quite his own. I fear that we shall never exchange words again, and I know that he will never come into this room again for a pleasant hour. . . .

August 13, 1891.

. . . Well, dear child, all is over, as you know, and many letters have been called for in consequence. As I shall not fail to have said before — for I have been repeating it to myself in a reproachful way — I had my last hour and my last word with him the day before I came to Stockbridge, and did not know it. And it could not have been better had I known it, the wise may say; but I wish I had had a little more fear and had put a secret farewell into my good-bye. He had only three days of rational life after that. Now we know the precise cause of his sufferings, it is a wonder that he didn't suffer much more. Poor Mabel's behavior was exactly fit: all tenderness and affection, some tears, but no abandonment. I became much attached to her in the course of a few weeks and she seems to have been drawn to me. The decline was very rapid in the last few days. Mabel has one smile to hoard which he gave her on Monday. I have been looking over his letters today. He sometimes had a woman's fond way of phrasing, though he was not effusive. Even as ambassador he sometimes signs himself "Jamie." It is certain that somewhat most precious is gone from my world. . . .

. . . I am not uncheerful. Just now I feel my loss, our loss. I am glad to have him released from pain and the inability to do what he had in hand or thought. But he would have liked to live, and his mind was in excellent working order. He was not of the sceptic sort, neither was he of the blind believers. He was a poet and had his revelations as such. I believe that he lives on. Think always thus. Can we imagine a possible happiness that the divinity cannot conceive? Can we wish more than he to effectuate the happiness we can conceive? He does not lack power; that you may know by looking at the skies. For the present we are in the dark. If light can deceive, wherefore not life? My dearest M., you are one of my evidences. James L. was another. . . .

This was written on the day before Lowell's funeral. In the *Letters of William James* a note written by him on the next day is found: '*Aug.* 14. "Lowell's funeral at mid-day. . . . Went to Child's to say good-bye, and found Walcott, Howells, Cranch, etc. Poor dear old Child! We drank a glass standing to the hope of seeing Lowell again." ' [49]

And now once more to Child:

Sunday, August 23, 1891.

. . . The world will never be the same again without J. R. L. It was not such a loss as you had in ——. . . . But it is a loss that I feel all the time. I could resort to him for a certain kind of sympathy which I could have from no other man. Some day when we are together I will show you some of his letters. They are mostly brief ones, but they are so kind. I love to look at them. . . .

There is a thing which I regret, and that is J. R. L. did not die in his full mind. Could I have sat by his bed or his chair, his lamp slowly declining, and could we have talked of the other life, in which we both believed, could I have read him cherished places from the Bible, there would have been much happiness to remember from the last days. But there is much from earlier days. He was a man without stain, no meanness, no cruelty, no vileness, no littleness, noble and good and innocent. I wish I could be with you two or three days to talk all this over, with love and blessing, and what it all points to.

I am going on with my work in an easy way. I can't say that I care so much about it without J. R. L., who has done much for me. He would have been so much pleased to have it all nicely finished up. He could take the fine points in a ballad. They seem stale. I go back to the fine ones at times and sing them and cry over them like the old world. . . .

December 17, 1891.

. . . The 22nd of February I am planning to have a solemn music in the afternoon in memory of J. R. L. There will perhaps be a choir of 50 boys, besides a fine choir of men's voices. So far I have chosen the most exquisite

[49] *The Letters of William James*, ed. Henry James (Boston, 1920), I, 315, n.

83

of Cherubini's Requiems, with the Kyrie pertaining to the same mass, a very beautiful Sanctus of Gounod, and perhaps Händel's famous Largo (with proper words). It will be a public performance, but I shall send tickets to all the nice people about here, and friends of the College. Now if *you* were making a visit northward at that time! . . .

. . . I will tell you more about the commemorative service by and by. I wish it were right to have a whole Mass of Cherubini's. My dear J. R. L. was no unbeliever, but he was not of Rome. If anything could carry me over it would be the Masses. They ought to be true; they must be true to something that cannot be lightly esteemed. . . .

Wednesday Morning, February 3, 1892.

. . . A few minutes ago our choir-master was here to consult about one piece more for the 22nd. Great pains have been taken, and the music is very good. . . . I think I gave you a list of the pieces. Anyway I will give you the whole programme, as we have it now, *fixed*.

> Requiem — Cherubini — C Minor Mass.
> Miserere — Allegri (part).
> Pie Jesu, Agnus Dei, Cherubini — D Minor Mass.
> Palestrina, Omnes amici.
> Mendelssohn — Beati mortui.
> Christopher Bach — Motet.
> Gounod — Sanctus.
> Mendelssohn — Periti autem.
> Schubert — Great is Jehovah.
> Organ.

I do not doubt that the music will be lovely, the performance I mean, for the music is of the highest style. . . .

Wednesday Evening, March 2, 1892.

. . . We have heard a great deal of satisfaction and approbation expressed about our commemoration of James Lowell. To me it was a very serious thing, and therefore when friends have declared it a "success" or the like, I have not felt entirely in harmony with them. But people generally have been more felicitous in their terms, and really have exceeded every expectation. The absolute silence from the first note of the organ to the last of the Sanctus showed where their thoughts and what their moods were. I have been much pleased by many saying that the service was the most fitting thing that could be, and much the more that not a word was said. . . .

So let this story of the scholar-friends come to its end. Surely it is another fitting thing that not a word more is now to be said.